D22

THE
STORY OF UTOPIAS

BY

LEWIS MUMFORD

With an Introduction
by
HENDRIK WILLEM VAN LOON

"A Map of the World that
does not include Utopia is not
worth even glancing at. . . ."

BONI AND LIVERIGHT
PUBLISHERS   NEW YORK

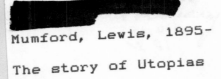

Printed in the United States of America

ACKNOWLEDGMENTS

The first outline of this book dates back ten years; and
since then I have woven it and rewoven it in my mind. The
actual work of composition was started by a suggestion
from Mr. Van Wyck Brooks; and without Mr. Brooks'
encouragement I should perhaps never have begun or
carried through the task. The general background of ideas
has been heavily colored by my contacts with Professor
Patrick Geddes, through his books and by correspondence;
and I owe a debt to him I have not always been able to
acknowledge in direct reference or in quotation marks. I
take the opportunity here to express the hearty gratitude
which might otherwise have been conveyed in the more
archaic form of a dedication.

In the revision of the MS. I have been blessed with the
generous advice and criticism of a number of friends; in
particular, Mr. Clarence Britten, Mr. Herbert Feis, Mr.
Geroid Robinson, and Miss Sophia Wittenberg, each of
whom performed a unique service. To Messrs. Victor
Branford and Alexander Farquharson of the Sociological
Society of Great Britain I am indebted for many
pertinent suggestions. My thanks are also due to the
editors of The Freeman for permission to use extracts from
two articles: Towards a Humanist Synthesis and Beauty
and the Picturesque. Finally, Mr. Hendrik van Loon's
friendly interest calls for a departing beam of gratitude.

LEWIS MUMFORD.

New York City.

CONTENTS

Introduction by Hendrik Willem van Loon, Ph.D.

CHAPTER ONE

CHAPTER TWO

CHAPTER THREE

CHAPTER FOUR

CHAPTER FIVE

CHAPTER SIX

CONTENTS

CHAPTER SEVEN

CHAPTER EIGHT

CHAPTER NINE

CHAPTER TEN

CHAPTER ELEVEN

CHAPTER TWELVE

INTRODUCTION

I⊤ is a sunny day and I am sitting on the top of a mountain.

Until this morning, it had been the mountain of a fairy story that was twenty centuries old.

Now, it is a mighty hill and I can feel its warm coat of white reindeer-moss, and if I were willing to stretch out my hand, I could pluck the red berries that are in full bloom.

A hundred years from now it will be gone.

For it is really a large chunk of pure iron, dumped by a playful Providence in the very heart of Lapland.

Do you remember an old tale of Norse mythology? How somewhere, far in the north, there stood a high peak of iron, which was a hundred miles high and a hundred miles wide? And how a little bird came to it once every thousand years to sharpen its beak? And how, when the mountain was gone, a single second of all eternity would have passed by?

I heard it told as a child.

I remembered it always, and I told it to my own boys when they began to learn history. It seemed the invention of some prehistoric Hans Christian Andersen. It belonged to the imaginary scenery of our dreams.

The story has come true, and I have found my old mountain where I least expected it.

To make the cycle of coincidence perfect, this hill was named after a bird. The Lapp, with a fine sense of sound, called the ptarmigan "Kiru." Kirunavaara no longer hears the shrill "kiru-kiru" of rising birds. Twice a day it listens to the terrific detonation of half a hundred charges of dynamite.

Then it is shaken by the little trains which carry the rock to the valley.

In the evening, it sees the lights of the large electric engines which hoist the valuable metal across the arctic wilderness of Lake Tornotrask.

Two months later, the ore has been melted and worked into those modern articles of trade which go by the name of bridges and automobiles and ships and apartment houses and a thousand other things which once promised to elevate man from the ranks of the beasts of burden.

What has become of that promise, the survivors of the last eight years know with great if gruesome accuracy.

Even the humble Lapp has heard of the great upheaval, and has asked why the white people should kill each other when the whole world was full of reindeer and when God has given us the hills and the plains so that forever there should be food enough for the long days of summer and the longer nights of the endless winter.

But the ways of the Lapp are not the ways of the white man. These simple followers of a pure and much undiluted nature follow the even tenor of their ways as their ancestors did, five and ten thousand years ago.

We, on the other hand, have our engines and we have our railroad trains and we have our factories and we cannot get rid of these iron servants without destroying the very basis of our civilization. We may hate these ungainly companions, but we need them. In time to come, we shall know how to be their masters. Then Plato shall give us a revised Republic where all the houses are heated by steam and where all the dishes are washed by electricity.

We are not suffering from too much machinery, but from too little. For let there be enough iron servants and more of us shall be able to sit on the tops of mountains and stare into the blue sky and waste valuable hours, imagining the things that ought to be.

[x]

INTRODUCTION

The Old Testament used to call such people prophets. They raised strange cities of their hearts' delight, which should be based exclusively upon righteousness and piety. But the greatest of all their prophets the Jews killed to make a Roman holiday.

The Greeks knew such wise men as philosophers. They allowed them great freedom and rejoiced in the mathematical precision with which their intellectual leaders mapped out those theoretical roads which were to lead mankind from chaos to an ordered state of society.

The Middle Ages insisted with narrow persistence upon the Kingdom of Heaven as the only possible standard for a decent Christian Utopia.

They crushed all those who dared to question the positive existence of such a future state of glory and content. They built it of stone and precious metals, but neglected the spiritual fundament.

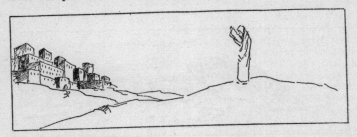

And so it perished.

The sixteenth and seventeenth centuries fought many bitter wars to decide the exact nature of a whitewashed Paradise, erected upon the crumbling ruins of the mediæval church.

The eighteenth century saw the Promised Land lying just across the terrible bulwark of stupidity and superstition, which a thousand years of clerical selfishness had erected for its own protection and safety.

There followed a mighty battle to crush the infamy of ignorance and bring about an era of well-balanced reason.

Unfortunately, a few enthusiasts carried the matter a trifle too far.

Napoleon, realist-in-chief of all time, brought the world back to the common ground of solid facts.

Our own generation drew the logical conclusion of the Napoleonic premises.

Behold the map of Europe and see how well we have wrought.

INTRODUCTION

For alas! this world needs Utopias as it needs fairy stories. It does not matter so much where we are going, as long as we are making consciously for some definite goal. And a Utopia, however strange or fanciful, is the only possible beacon upon the uncharted seas of the distant future.

It encourages us in our efforts. Sometimes the light is hidden by the clouds and for a moment we may lose our way. Then the faint light once more breaks through the darkness and we press forward with new courage.

And when life is dull and meaningless (the main curse of all existence) we find consolation in the fact that a hundred years from now, our children shall reach the shore for which we were bound when we ourselves left the bridge and were lowered to the peaceful bottom of the ocean.

And now the sun has gone down and a chill wind blows from Kebnekajse, where the wild geese of little Nils Holgerson live amidst the endless silence of the eternal snow. Soon the top shall be hidden in the mist and I shall have to find my way back by the noise of the steam shovels, plying their elephantine trade at the foot of the first terrace.

The mountain of my fairy story once more will be the profitable investment of a Company of Iron-mongers.

[xii]

INTRODUCTION

But that does not matter.

Lewis Mumford, for whom I am writing this, will understand what I mean.

And I shall be content.

Kiruna, Lapland,
     14 Sept., 1922.

Hendrik Willem van Loon

CHAPTER ONE

How the will-to-utopia causes men to live in two
worlds, and how, therefore, we re-read the Story of
Utopias—the other half of the Story of Mankind.

THE STORY OF UTOPIAS

CHAPTER ONE

1

UTOPIA has long been another name for the unreal
and the impossible. We have set utopia over against
the world. As a matter of fact, it is our utopias that
make the world tolerable to us: the cities and mansions
that people dream of are those in which they finally
live. The more that men react upon their environment
and make it over after a human pattern, the more con-
tinuously do they live in utopia; but when there is a
breach between the world of affairs and the overworld
of utopia, we become conscious of the part that the
will-to-utopia has played in our lives, and we see our
utopia as a separate reality.

It is the separate reality of utopia that we are
going to explore in the course of this book—Utopia
as a world by itself, divided into ideal commonwealths,
with all its communities clustered into proud cities,
aiming bravely at the good life.

This discussion of ideal commonwealths gets its form
and its color from the time in which it is written.
Plato's Republic dates from the period of social dis-
integration which followed the Peloponnesian War;
and some of its mordant courage is probably derived
from the hopelessness of conditions that came under

[11]

Plato's eye. It was in the midst of a similar period of
disorder and violence that Sir Thomas More laid the
foundations for his imaginary commonwealth: Utopia
was the bridge by which he sought to span the gap between the old order of the Middle Age, and the new
interests and institutions of the Renascence.

In presenting this history and criticism of utopias we
are perhaps being pulled by the same interests that led
Plato and More onwards, for it is only after the storm
that we dare to look for the rainbow. Our fall into a
chasm of disillusion has stimulated us to discuss in
a more thorough way the ultimate goods, the basic
aims, the whole conception of the "good life" by which,
in modern times, we have been guided. In the midst of
the tepid and half-hearted discussions that continue
to arise out of prohibition laws and strikes and "peace"
conferences let us break in with the injunction to talk
about fundamentals—consider Utopia!

2

Man walks with his feet on the ground and his head
in the air; and the history of what has happened on
earth—the history of cities and armies and of all the
things that have had body and form—is only one-half
the Story of Mankind.

In every age, the external scenery in which the human
drama has been framed has remained pretty much the
same. There have been fluctuations in climate and
changes in terrain; and at times a great civilization,
like that of the Mayas in Central America, has arisen
where now only a thick net of jungle remains; but the
hills around Jerusalem are the hills that David saw;

and during the historic period the drowning of a city in the Netherlands or the rise of a shifting bank of real estate along the coast of New Jersey is little more than the wearing off of the paint or a crack in the plaster. What we call the material world constantly changes, it goes without saying: mountains are stript of trees and become wastes, deserts are plowed with water and become gardens. The main outlines, however, hold their own remarkably well; and we could have travelled better in Roman days with a modern map than with the best chart Ptolemy could have offered us.

If the world in which men live were the world as it is known to the physical geographer, we should have a pretty simple time of it. We might follow Whitman's advice, and live as the animals, and stop whining for all time about our sins and imperfections.

What makes human history such an uncertain and fascinating story is that man lives in two worlds—the world within and the world without—and the world within men's heads has undergone ·transformations which have disintegrated material things with the power and rapidity of radium. I shall take the liberty of calling this inner world our idolum (ido'lum) or world of ideas. The word "ideas" is not used here precisely in the ordinary sense. I use it rather to stand for what the philosophers would call the subjective world, what the theologians would perhaps call the spiritual world; and I mean to include in it all the philosophies, fantasies, rationalizations, projections, images, and opinions in terms of which people pattern their behavior. This world of ideas, in the case of scientific truths, for example, sometimes has a rough correspondence with what people call the world; but it is important to note that it has contours of its own which are quite independent of the material environment.

Now the physical world is a definite, inescapable thing. Its limits are narrow and obvious. On occasion, if your impulse is sufficiently strong, you can leave the land for the sea, or go from a warm climate into a cool one; but you cannot cut yourself off from the physical environment without terminating your life. For good or ill, you must breathe air, eat food, drink water; and the penalties for refusing to meet these conditions are inexorable. Only a lunatic would refuse to recognize this physical environment; it is the substratum of our daily lives.

But if the physical environment is the earth, the world of ideas corresponds to the heavens. We sleep under the light of stars that have long since ceased to exist, and we pattern our behavior by ideas which have no reality as soon as we cease to credit them. Whilst it holds together this world of ideas—this idolum—is almost as sound, almost as real, almost as inescapable as the bricks of our houses or the asphalt beneath our feet. The "belief" that the world was flat was once upon a time more important than the "fact" that it was round; and that belief kept the sailors of the medieval world from wandering out of sight of land as effectively as would a string of gunboats or floating mines. An idea is a solid fact, a theory is a solid fact, a superstition is a solid fact as long as people continue to regulate their actions in terms of the idea, theory, or superstition; and it is none the less solid because it is conveyed as an image or a breath of sound.

[14]

3

This world of ideas serves many purposes. Two of them bear heavily upon our investigation of utopia. On one hand the pseudo-environment or idolum is a substitute for the external world; it is a sort of house of refuge to which we flee when our contacts with "hard facts" become too complicated to carry through or too rough to face. On the other hand, it is by means of the idolum that the facts of the everyday world are brought together and assorted and sifted, and a new sort of reality is projected back again upon the external world. One of these functions is escape or compensation; it seeks an immediate release from the difficulties or frustrations of our lot. The other attempts to provide a condition for our release in the future. The utopias that correspond to these two functions I shall call the utopias of escape and the utopias of reconstruction. The first leaves the external world the way it is; the second seeks to change it so that one may have intercourse with it on one's own terms. In one we build impossible castles in the air; in the other we consult a surveyor and an architect and a mason and proceed to build a house which meets our essential needs; as well as houses made of stone and mortar are capable of meeting them.

4

Why, however, should we find it necessary to talk about utopia and the world of ideas at all? Why should we not rest secure in the bosom of the material environment, without flying off into a region apparently beyond space and time? Well, the alternative

[15]

before us is not whether we shall live in the real world
or dream away our time in utopia; for men are so
constituted that only by a deliberate discipline—such
as that followed by a Hindu ascetic or an American
business man—can one or the other world be abolished
from consciousness. The genuine alternative for most
of us is that between an aimless utopia of escape and
a purposive utopia of reconstruction. One way or the
other, it seems, in a world so full of frustrations as
the "real" one, we must spend a good part of our
mental lives in utopia.

Nevertheless this needs a qualification. It is plain
that certain types of people have no need for private
utopias and that certain communities seem to be without them. The savages of the Marquesas whom Her-
mann Melville described seem to have had such a jolly
and complete adjustment to their environment that,
except for the raids of hostile tribes—and this turned
out to be chiefly sport which only whetted their appetites for the feast that followed—everything needed
for a good life at the South Sea level could be obtained
by direct attack. The Marquesans had no need to
dream of a happier existence; they had only to grab it.

At times, during childhood perhaps, life has the
same sort of completeness; and without doubt there are
many mature people who have manufactured out of
their limitations a pretty adequate response to a narrow environment; and have let it go at that. Such
people feel no need for utopia. As long as they can
keep their contacts restricted, only a deliberate raid
from the outside world would create such a need. They
are like the sick man in the parable of the Persian poet,
whose only desire was that he might desire something;

[16]

and there is no particular reason to envy them. People who will not venture out into the open sea pay the penalty of never having looked into the bright eyes of danger; and at best they know but half of life. What such folk might call the good life is simply not good enough. We cannot be satisfied with a segment of existence, no matter how safely we may be adjusted to it, when with a little effort we can trace the complete circle.

But there have been few regions, few social orders, and few people in which the adjustment has not been incomplete. In the face of perpetual difficulties and obstructions—the wind and the weather and the impulses of other men and customs that have long outlived their use—there are three ways, roughly, in which a man may react. He may run away. He may try to hold his own. He may attack. Looking around at our contemporaries who have survived the war, it is fairly evident that most of them are in the first stage of panic and despair. In an interesting article on The Dénouement of Nihilism, Mr. Edward Townsend Booth characterized the generation born in the late eighties as suffering a complete paralysis of will, or else, "if any initiative remains to them, they emigrate to Europe or the South Sea Islands, or crawl off into some quiet corner of the United States—but most of them continue where they were stricken in a state of living death."

Speaking more generally, running away does not always mean a physical escape, nor does an "attack" necessarily mean doing something practical "on the spot." Let us use Dr. John Dewey's illustration and suppose that a man is denied intercourse with his friends at a distance. One kind of reaction is for him to "imagine" meeting his friends, and going through, in fantasy, a whole ritual of meeting, repartee, and discussion. The other kind of reaction, as Dr. Dewey says, is to see what conditions must be met in order to cement distant friends, and then invent the telephone. The so-called extrovert, the type of man who has no need for utopias, will satisfy his desire by talking to the nearest human being. ("He may try to hold his own.") But it is fairly plain that the extrovert, from the very weakness and inconstancy of his aims, is incapable of contributing anything but "good nature" to the good life of the community; and in his hands both art and invention would probably come to an end.

Now putting aside the extrovert, we find that the two remaining types of reaction have expressed themselves in all the historic utopias. It is perhaps well that we should see them first in their normal, everyday setting, before we set out to explore the ideal commonwealths of the past.

More or less, we have all had glimpses of the utopia of escape: it is raised and it collapses and it is built up again almost daily. In the midst of the clanking machinery of a paper factory I have come across a moving picture actress's portrait, stuck upon an inoperative part of the machine; and it was not hard to reconstruct the private utopia of the wretch who minded the levers, or to picture the world into which he had fled from the roar and throb and muck of the machinery about him. What man has not had this utopia from the dawn of adolescence onwards—the desire to possess and be possessed by a beautiful woman?

Perhaps for the great majority of men and women that small, private Utopia is the only one for which they feel a perpetual, warm interest; and ultimately every other utopia must be translatable to them in some such intimate terms. Their conduct would tell us as much if their words did not confess it. They leave their bleak office buildings and their grimy factories, and night after night they pour into the cinema theater in order that they may live for a while in a land populated by beautiful, flirtatious women and tender, lusty men. Small wonder that the great and powerful religion founded by Mahomet puts that utopia in the very foreground of the hereafter! In a sense, this is the most elementary of utopias; for, on the interpretation of the analytical psychologist, it carries with it the deep longing to return to and remain at rest in the mother's womb—the one perfect environment which all the machinery and legislation of an eager world has never been able to reproduce.

In its most elemental state, this utopia of escape calls for a complete breach with the butcher, the baker, the grocer, and the real, limited, imperfect people that flutter around us. In order to make it more perfect, we eliminate the butcher and baker and transport ourselves to a self-sufficient island in the South Seas. For the most part, of course, this is an idle dream, and if we do not grow out of it, we must at any rate thrust other conditions into it; but for a good many of us, idleness without a dream is the only alternative. Out of such fantasies of bliss and perfection, which do not endure in real life even when they occasionally bloom into existence, our art and literature have very largely grown. It is hard to conceive of a social order so complete and

[19]

satisfactory that it would rob us of the necessity of having recourse, from time to time, to an imaginary world in which our sufferings could be purged or our delights heightened. Even in the great idyll painted by William Morris, women are fickle and lovers are disappointed; and when the "real" world becomes a little too hard and too sullen to face, we must take refuge, if we are to recover our balance, into another world which responds more perfectly to our deeper interests and desires—the world of literature.

Once we have weathered the storm, it is dangerous to remain in the utopia of escape; for it is an enchanted island, and to remain there is to lose one's capacity for dealing with things as they are. The girl who has felt Prince Charming's caresses too long will be repulsed by the clumsy embraces of the young man who takes her to the theater and wonders how the deuce he is going to pay the rent if they spend more than a week on their honeymoon. Moreover, life is too easy in the utopia of escape, and too blankly perfect—there is nothing to sharpen your teeth upon. It is not for this that men have gone into the jungle to hunt beasts and have cajoled the grasses and roots to be prolific, and have defied, in little open boats, the terror of the wind and sea. Our daily diet must have more roughage in it than these daydreams will give us if we are not to become debilitated.

In the course of our journey into utopia we shall remain a little while in these utopias of escape; but we shall not bide there long. There are plenty of them, and they dot the waters of our imaginary world as the islands that Ulysses visited dotted the Ægean Sea. These utopias however belong to the department of pure literature, and in that department they occupy but a minor place. We could dispense with the whole lot of them, bag and baggage, in exchange for another Anna Karenin or The Brothers Karamazov.

5

The second kind of utopia which we shall encounter is the utopia of reconstruction.

The first species represents, the analytical psychologist would tell us, a very primitive kind of thinking, in which we follow the direction of our desires without taking into account any of the limiting conditions which we should have to confront if we came back to earth and tried to realize our wishes in practical affairs. It is a vague and messy and logically inconsequent series of images which color up and fade, which excite us and leave us cold, and which—for the sake of the respect our neighbors have for our ability to add a ledger or plane a piece of wood—we had better confine to the strange box of records we call our brain.

The second type of utopia may likewise be colored by primitive desires and wishes; but these desires and wishes have come to reckon with the world in which they seek realization. The utopia of reconstruction is what its name implies: a vision of a reconstituted environment which is better adapted to the nature and aims of the human beings who dwell within it than the actual one; and not merely better adapted to their actual nature, but better fitted to their possible developments. If the first utopia leads backward into the utopian's ego, the second leads outward—outward into the world.

By a reconstructed environment I do not mean merely a physical thing. I mean, in addition, a new set of habits, a fresh scale of values, a different net of

[21]

relationships and institutions, and possibly—for almost all utopias emphasize the factor of breeding—an alteration of the physical and mental characteristics of the people chosen, through education, biological selection, and so forth. The reconstructed environment which all the genuine utopians seek to contrive is a reconstruction of both the physical world and the idolum. It is in this that the utopian distinguishes himself from the practical inventor and the industrialist. Every attempt that has been made to domesticate animals, cultivate plants, dredge rivers, dig ditches, and in modern times, apply the energy of the sun to mechanical instruments, has been an effort to reconstruct the environment; and in many cases the human advantage has been plain. It is not for the utopian to despise Prometheus who brought the fire or Franklin who captured the lightning. As Anatole France says: "Without the Utopians of other times, men would still live in caves, miserable and naked. It was Utopians who traced the lines of the first city. . . . Out of generous dreams come beneficial realities. Utopia is the principle of all progress, and the essay into a better future."

Our physical reconstructions however have been limited; they have touched chiefly the surfaces of things. The result is that people live in a modern physical environment and carry in their minds an odd assortment of spiritual relics from almost every other age, from that of the primitive, taboo-ridden savage, to the energetic Victorian disciples of Gradgrind and Bounderby. As Mr. Hendrik van Loon pithily says: "A human being with the mind of a sixteenth century tradesman driving a 1921 Rolls-Royce is still a human

being with the mind of a sixteenth century tradesman."
The problem is fundamentally a human problem. The
more completely man is in control of physical nature,
the more urgently we must ask ourselves what under
the heavens is to move and guide and keep in hand the
controller. This problem of an ideal, a goal, an end—
even if the aim persist in shifting as much as the magnetic north pole—is a fundamental one to the utopian.

Except in the writings of the utopians, and this
is an important point to notice in our travels through
utopia, the reconstruction of the material environment
and the reconstitution of the mental framework of the
creatures who inhabit it, have been kept in two different compartments. One compartment is supposed to
belong to the practical man; the other to the idealist.
The first was something whose aims could be realized
in the Here and Now; the other was postponed very
largely to the sweet by-and-bye. Neither the practical
man nor the idealist has been willing to admit that he
has been dealing with a single problem; that each has
been treating the faces of a single thing as if they were
separate.

Here is where the utopia of reconstruction wins
hands down. It not merely pictures a whole world, but
it faces every part of it at the same time. We shall
not examine the classic utopias without becoming
conscious of their weaknesses, their sometimes disturbing idiosyncrasies. It is important at present that we
should realize their virtues; and should start on our
journey without the feeling of disparagement which
the word utopian usually calls up in minds that have
been seduced by Macaulay's sneer that he would rather
have an acre in Middlesex than a principality in utopia.

Finally, be convinced about the reality of utopia.
All that has happened in what we call human history—
unless it has left a building or a book or some other
record of itself—is just as remote and in a sense just
as mythical as the mysterious island which Raphael
Hythloday, scholar and sailor, described to Sir Thomas
More. A good part of human history is even more
insubstantial: the Icarians who lived only in the mind
of Étienne Cabet, or the Freelanders who dwelt within
the imagination of a dry little Austrian economist, have
had more influence upon the lives of our contemporaries
than the Etruscan people who once dwelt in Italy, although the Etruscans belong to what we call the real
world, and the Freelanders and Icarians inhabited—
Nowhere.

Nowhere may be an imaginary country, but News
from Nowhere is real news. The world of ideas, beliefs, fantasies, projections, is (I must emphasize
again) just as real whilst it is acted upon as the post
which Dr. Johnson kicked in order to demonstrate that
it was solid. The man who wholly respects the rights
of property is kept out of his neighbor's field perhaps
even more effectively than the man who is merely for-
bidden entrance by a no-trespass sign. In sum, we
cannot ignore our utopias. They exist in the same
way that north and south exist; if we are not familiar
with their classical statements we at least know them
as they spring to life each day in our own minds. We
can never reach the points of the compass; and so no
doubt we shall never live in utopia; but without the
magnetic needle we should not be able to travel intelli-

[24]

gently at all. It is absurd to dispose of utopia by saying that it exists only on paper. The answer to this is: precisely the same thing may be said of the architect's plans for a house, and houses are none the worse for it.

We must lose our sense of remoteness and severity in setting out on this exploration of ideal commonwealths, as some of the fine minds of the past have pictured them. Our ideals are not something that we can set apart from the main facts of our existence, as our grandmothers sometimes set the cold, bleak, and usually moldy parlor apart from the living rooms of the house: on the contrary, the things we dream of tend consciously or unconsciously to work themselves out in the pattern of our daily lives. Our utopias are just as human and warm and jolly as the world out of which they are born. Looking out from the top of a high tenement, over the housetops of Manhattan, I can see a pale tower with its golden pinnacle gleaming through the soft morning haze; and for a moment all the harsh and ugly lines in the landscape have disappeared. So in looking at our utopias. We need not abandon the real world in order to enter these realizable worlds; for it is out of the first that the second are always coming.

Finally, an anticipation and a warning. In our journey through the utopias of the past we shall not rest content when we have traversed the whole territory between Plato and the latest modern writer. If the story of utopia throws any light upon the story of mankind it is this: our utopias have been pitifully weak and inadequate; and if they have not exercised enough practical influence upon the course of affairs, it is because, as Viola Paget says in Gospels of Anarchy, they were simply not good enough. We travel through utopia only in order to get beyond utopia: if we leave the domains of history when we enter the gates of Plato's Republic, we do so in order to re-enter more effectively the dusty midday traffic of the contemporary world. So our study of the classic utopias will be followed by an examination of certain social myths and partial utopias that have played an important part in the affairs of the Western World during the last few centuries. In the end, I promise, I shall make no attempt to present another utopia; it will be enough to survey the foundations upon which others may build.

In the meanwhile, our ship is about to set sail; and we shall not heave anchor again until we reach the coasts of Utopia.

CHAPTER TWO

How the Greeks lived in a New World, and utopia
seemed just round the corner. How Plato, in the
Republic, is chiefly concerned with what will hold
the ideal city together.

CHAPTER TWO

1

BEFORE the great empires of Rome and Macedonia
began to spread their camps through the length and
breadth of the Mediterranean world, there was a time
when the vision of an ideal city seems to have been
uppermost in the minds of a good many men. Just as
the wide expanse of unsettled territory in America
caused the people of eighteenth century Europe to
think of building a civilization in which the errors and
vices and superstitions of the old world might be left
behind, so the sparsely settled coasts of Italy, Sicily,
and the Ægean Islands, and the shores of the Black
Sea, must have given men the hope of being able to
turn over a fresh page.

Those years between six hundred and three hundred
B. C. were city-building years for the parent cities of
Greece. The city of Miletus is supposed to have be-
gotten some three hundred cities, and many of its fellows were possibly not less fruitful. Since new cities
could be founded there was plenty of chance for varia-
tion and experiment; and those who dreamed of a more,
generous social order could set their hands and wits to
making a better start "from the bottom up."

Of all the plans and reconstruction programs that
must have been put forward during these centuries,
only a scant handful remains. Aristotle tells us about
an ideal state designed by one, Phaleas, who believed

[29]

like Mr. Bernard Shaw in a complete equality of property; and from Aristotle, too, we learn of another utopia which was described by the great architect, city planner, and sociologist—Hippodamus. Hippodamus was one of the first city planners known to history, and he achieved fame in the ancient world by designing cities on the somewhat monotonous checkerboard design we know so well in America. He realized, apparently, that a city was something more than a collection of houses, streets, markets, and temples; and so, whilst he was putting the physical town to rights, he concerned himself with the more basic problem of the social order. If it adds at all to our sense of reality in going through utopia, let me confess that it is ultimately through the inspiration and example of another Hippodamus—Patrick Geddes, the town planner for Jerusalem and many other cities—that this book about utopias came to be written. In many ways the distance between Geddes and Aristotle or Hippodamus seems much less than that which separates Geddes and Herbert Spencer.

When we look at the utopias that Phaleas and Hippodamus and Aristotle have left us, and compare them with the Republic of Plato, the differences between them melt into insignificance and their likenesses are apparent. It is for this reason that I shall confine our examination of the Greek utopia to that which Plato set forth in the Republic, and qualified and broadened in The Laws, The Statesman, and Critias.

2

Plato's Republic dates roughly from the time of that long and disastrous war which Athens fought with

Sparta. In the course of such a war, amid the bombast that patriotic citizens give way to, the people who keep their senses are bound to get pretty well acquainted with their enemy. If you will take the trouble to examine Plutarch's account of the Laws of Lycurgus and Mr. Alfred Zimmern's magnificent description of the Greek Commonwealth you will see how Sparta and Athens form the web and woof of the Republic—only it is an ideal Sparta and an ideal Athens that Plato has in mind.

It is well to remember that Plato wrote in the midst of defeat; a great part of his region, Attica, had been devastated and burned; and he must have felt that makeshift and reform were quite futile when a Peloponnesian war could make the bottom drop out of his world. To Plato an ill-designed ship of state required more than the science of navigation to pull it through stormy waters: if it was in danger of perpetually foundering, it seemed high time to go back to the shipyards and inquire into the principles upon which it had been put together. In such a mood, I suggest parenthetically, we today will turn again to fundamentals.

3

In describing his ideal community Plato, like a trained workman, begins with his physical foundations. So far from putting his utopia in a mythical island of Avilion, where falls not hail nor rain nor any snow, it is plain that Plato was referring repeatedly to the soil in which Athens was planted, and to the economic life which grew out of that soil. Since he was speaking to his own countrymen, he could let a good many things pass for common knowledge which we, as strangers, must look into more carefully in order to have a firmer sense of his utopian realities. Let it be understood that in discussing the physical side of the Republic, I am drawing from Aristotle as well as Plato, and from such modern Greek scholars as Messrs. Zimmern, Myres, and Murray.

Nowadays when we talk about a state we think of an expanse of territory, to begin with, so broad that we should in most cases be unable to see all its boundaries if we rose five miles above the ground on a clear day. Even if the country is a little one, like the Netherlands or Belgium, it is likely to have possessions that are thousands of miles away; and we think of these distant possessions and of the homeland as part and parcel of the state. There is scarcely any conceivable way in which a Dutchman in Rotterdam, let us say, possesses the Island of Java: he does not live on the island, he is not acquainted with the inhabitants, he does not share their ideas or customs. His interest in Java, if he have an interest at all, is an interest in sugar, coffee, taxes, or missions. His state is not a commonwealth in the sense that it is a common possession.

To the Greek of Plato's time, on the contrary, the commonwealth was something he actively shared with his fellow citizens. It was a definite parcel of land whose limits he could probably see from any convenient hilltop; and those who lived within those limits had common gods to worship, common theaters and gymnasia, and a multitude of common interests that could be satisfied only by their working together, playing together, thinking together. Plato could probably not have conceived of a community with civilized pretensions in which the population was distributed at the rate of ten per square mile; and if he visited such a territory he would surely have said that the people were barbarians—men whose way of living unfitted them for the graces and duties of citizenship.

Geographically speaking, then, the ideal commonwealth was a city-region; that is, a city which was surrounded by enough land to supply the greater part of the food needed by the inhabitants; and placed convenient to the sea.

Let us stand on a high hill and take a look at this city region; the sort of view that Plato himself might have obtained on some clear spring morning when he climbed to the top of the Acropolis and looked down on the sleeping city, with the green fields and sear upland pastures on one side, and the sun glinting on the distant waters of the sea a few miles away.

It is a mountainous region, this Greece, and within a short distance from mountain top to sea there was compressed as many different kinds of agricultural and industrial life as one could single out in going down the Hudson valley from the Adirondack Mountains to New York Harbor. As the basis for his ideal city, whether Plato knew it or not, he had an "ideal" section of land in his mind—what the geographer calls the "valley section." He could not have gotten the various groups which were to be combined in his city, had they been settled in the beginning on a section of land like the coastal plain of New Jersey. It was peculiarly in Greece that such a variety of occupations could come together within a small area, beginning at the summit of the valley section with the evergreen trees and the woodcutter, going down the slope to the herdsman and

[33]

his flock of goats at pasture, along the valley bottom to the cultivator and his crops, until at length one reaches the river's mouth where the fisher pushes out to sea in his boat and the trader comes in with goods from other lands.

The great civilizations of the world have been nourished in such valley sections. We think of the river Nile and Alexandria; the Tiber and Rome, the Seine and Paris; and so on. It is interesting that our first great utopia should have had an "ideal" section of territory as its base.

4

In the economic foundations of the Republic, we look in vain for a recognition of the labor problem. Now the labor problem is a fundamental difficulty in our modern life; and it seems on the surface that Plato is a little highbrow and remote in the ease with which he gets over it. When we look more closely into the matter, however, and see the way in which men got their living in the "morning lands"—as the Germans call them—we shall find that the reason Plato does not offer a solution is that he was not, indeed, confronted by a problem.

Given a valley section which has not been ruthlessly stript of trees; given the arts of agriculture and herding; given a climate without dangerous extremes of heat and cold; given the opportunity to found new colonies when the old city-region is over-populated—and it is only by an exercise of ingenuity that a labor problem could be invented. A man might become a slave by military capture; he did not become a slave by being compelled, under threat of starvation, to tend a ma chine. The problem of getting a living was answered by nature as long as men were willing to put up with nature's conditions; and the groundwork of Plato's utopia, accordingly, is the simple agricultural life, the growing of wheat, barley, olives, and grapes, which had been fairly well mastered before he arrived on the scene. As long as the soil was not washed away and devitalized, the problem was not a hard one; and in order to solve it, Plato had only to provide that there should be enough territory to grow food on, and that the inhabitants must not let their wants exceed the bounties of nature.

Plato describes the foundations of his community with a few simple and masterly touches. Those who feel that there is something a little inhuman in his conception of the good life, when he is discussing the education and duties of the ruling classes, may well consider the picture that he paints for us here.

Plato's society arises out of the needs of mankind; because none of us is self-sufficing and all have many wants; and since there are many wants, many kinds of people must supply them. When all these helpers and partners and co-operators are gathered together in a city the body of inhabitants is termed a state; and so its members work and exchange goods with one another for their mutual advantage—the herdsman gets barley for his cheese and so on down to the complicated interchanges that occur in the city. What sort of physical life will arise out of this in the region that Plato describes?

Well, the people will "produce corn and wine and clothes and shoes and build houses for themselves. . . . They will work in summer commonly stript and barefoot, but in winter substantially clothed and shod. They will feed on barley and wheat, baking the wheat and kneading the flour, making noble puddings and loaves; these they will serve up on a mat of reeds or clean leaves; themselves reclining the while upon beds of yew or myrtle boughs. And they and their children will feast, drinking of the wine which they have made, wearing garlands on their heads, and having the praises of the gods on their lips, living in sweet society, and having a care that their families do not exceed their means; for they will have an eye to poverty or war."

So Socrates, in this dialogue on the Republic, describes to his hearers the essential physical elements of the good life. One of his hearers, Glaucon, asks him to elaborate it a little, for Socrates has limited himself to bare essentials. It is the same sort of objection, by the way, that M. Poincaré, the physicist, made to the philosophy of Tolstoy. Socrates answers that a good state would have the healthy constitution which he has just described; but that he has no objection to looking at an "inflamed constitution." What Socrates describes as an inflamed constitution is a mode of life which all the people of Western Europe and America at the present day—no matter what their religion, economic status, or political creed may be— believe in with almost a single mind; and so, although it is the opposite of Plato's ideal state, I go on to present it, for the light it throws on our own institutions and habits.

The unjust state comes into existence, says Plato through the mouth of Socrates, by the multiplication of wants and superfluities. As a result of increasing wants, we must enlarge our borders, for the original healthy state is too small. Now the city will fill up with a multitude of callings which go beyond those required by any natural want; there will be a host of parasites and "supers"; and our country, which was big enough to support the original inhabitants, will want a slice of our neighbor's land for pasture and tillage; and they will want a slice of ours if, like ourselves, they exceed the limits of necessity and give themselves up to the unlimited accumulation of wealth. "And then we shall go to war—that will be the next thing."

The sum of this criticism is that Plato saw clearly that an ideal community must have a common physical standard of living; and that boundless wealth or unlimited desires and gratifications had nothing to do with a good standard. The good was what was necessary; and what was necessary was not, essentially, many goods.

Like Aristotle, Plato wanted a mode of life which was neither impoverished nor luxurious: those who have read a little in Greek history will see that this Athenian ideal of the good life fell rather symbolically between Sparta and Corinth, between the cities which we associate respectively with a hard, military life and with a soft, super-sensuous æstheticism.

Should we moderate our wants or should we increase production? Plato had no difficulty in answering this question. He held that a reasonable man would moderate his wants; and that if he wished to live like a good farmer or a good philosopher he would not attempt to copy the expenditures of a vulgar gambler who has just made a corner in wheat, or a vulgar courtesan who has just made a conquest of the vulgar gambler who has made a corner in wheat. Wealth and poverty, said Plato, are the two causes of deterioration in the arts: both the workman and his works are likely to degenerate under the influence of either poverty or wealth, "for one is the parent of luxury and indolence, and the other of meanness and viciousness, and both of discontent."

Nor does Plato have one standard of living for his ruling classes and another for the common people. To each person he would give all the material things necessary for sustenance; and from each he would be prepared to strip all that was not essential. He realized that the possession of goods was not a means of getting happiness, but an effort to make up for a spiritually depauperate life: for Plato, happiness was what one could put into life and not what one could loot out of it: it was the happiness of the dancer rather than the happiness of the glutton. Plato pictured a community living a sane, continent, athletic, clear-eyed life; a community that would be always, so to say, within bounds. There is a horror of laxity and easy living in his Republic. His society was stripped for action. The fragrance that permeates his picture of the good life is not the heavy fragrance of rose-petals and incense falling upon languorous couches: it is the fragrance of the morning grass, and the scent of crushed mint or marjoram beneath the feet.

5

How big is Plato's community, how are the people divided, what are their relations? Now that we have discussed the lay out of the land, and have inquired into the physical basis of this utopia, we are ready to turn

[38]

our attention to the people; for it is out of the interaction of folk, work, and place that every community—
good or bad, real or fancied—exists and perpetuates
itself.

6

It follows almost inevitably from what we have said
of Plato's environment, that his ideal community was
not to be unlimited in population. Quite the contrary.
Plato said that "the city may increase to any size
which is consistent with its unity; that is the limit."
The modern political scientist, who lives within a national state of millions of people, and who thinks of
the greatness of states largely in terms of their population, has scoffed without mercy at the fact that Plato
limited his community to an arbitrary number, 5,040,
about the number that can be conveniently addressed
by a single orator. As a matter of fact there is nothing
ridiculous in Plato's definition: he was not speaking of
a horde of barbarians: he was laying down the foundations for an active polity of citizens: and it is plain
enough in all conscience that when you increase the
number of people in a community you decrease the
number of things that they can share in common. Plato
could not anticipate the wireless telephone and the
daily newspaper; still less would he have been likely
to exaggerate the difference which these instrumentali-
ties have made in the matters that most intimately
concern us; and when he set bounds to the population
his city would contain, he was anticipating by more
than two thousand years the verdict of modern town
planners like Mr. Raymond Unwin.

People are not the members of a community because

they live under the same system of political government or dwell in the same country. They become genuine citizens to the extent that they share certain institutions and ways of life with similarly educated people. Plato was primarily concerned with providing conditions which would make a community hold together without being acted upon by any external force—as the national state is acted upon today by war or the threat of war. This concern seems to underlie every line of the Republic. In attacking his problem, the business of supplying the physical wants of the city seemed relatively unimportant; and even though Greece in the time of Plato traded widely with the whole Mediterranean region, Plato did not mistake commercial unity for civic unity. Hence in his scheme of things the work of the farmer and the merchant and the trader was subordinate. The important thing to consider was the general conditions under which all the individuals and groups in a community might live together harmoniously. This is a long cry from the utopias of the nineteenth century, which we will examine later; and that is why it is important to understand Plato's point of view and follow his argument.

7

To Plato, a good community was like a healthy body; a harmonious exercise of every function was the condition of its strength and vitality. Necessarily then a good community could not be simply a collection of individuals, each one of whom insists upon some private and particular happiness without respect to the welfare and interests of his fellows. Plato believed that good-

[40]

ness and happiness—for he would scarcely admit that there was any distinct line of cleavage between these qualities—consisted in living according to nature; that is to say, in knowing one's self, in finding one's bent, and in fulfilling the particular work which one had the capacity to perform. The secret of a good community, therefore, if we may translate Plato's language into modern political slang, is the principle of function.

Every kind of work, says Plato, requires a particular kind of aptitude and training. If we wish to have good shoes, our shoes must be made by a shoemaker and not by a weaver; and in like manner, every man has some particular calling to which his genius leads him, and he finds a happiness for himself and usefulness to his fellows when he is employed in that calling. The good life must result when each man has a function to perform, and when all the necessary functions are adjusted happily to each other. The state is like the physical body. "Health is the creation of a natural order and government in the parts of the body, and the creation of disease is the creation of a state of things in which they are at variance with the natural order." The supreme virtue in the commonwealth is justice; namely, the due apportionment of work or function under the rule of "a place for every man and every man in his place."

Has any such society ever come into existence? Do not too hastily answer No. The ideal in Plato's mind is carried out point for point in the organization of a modern symphony orchestra.

Now Plato was not unaware that there were other formulas for happiness. He expressly points out however that in founding the Republic he does not wish to

[41]

make any single person or group happier beyond the rest; he desires rather that the whole city should be in the happiest condition. It would be easy enough "to array the husbandmen in rich and costly robes and to enjoin them to cultivate the ground only with a view to their pleasure," and so Plato might have conferred a spurious kind of felicity upon every individual. If this happened, however, there would be a brief period of ease and revelry before the whole works went to pot. In this Plato is a thoroughgoing realist: he is not looking for a short avenue of escape; he is ready to face the road with all its ups and downs, with its steep climbs as well as its wide vistas; and he does not think any the worse of life because he finds that its chief enjoyments rest in activity, and not, as the epicureans of all sorts have always believed, in a release from activity.

8

Plato arrives at his apportionment of functions by a method which is old-fashioned, and which anybody versed in modern psychology would regard as a "rationalization." Plato is trying to give a firm basis to the division of classes which he favored; and so he compares the community to a human being, possessed of the virtues of wisdom, valour, temperance, and justice. Each of these virtues Plato relates to a particular class of people.

Wisdom is appropriate to the rulers of the city. Thus arises the class of guardians.

Valour is the characteristic of the defenders of the city and hence a military class, called auxiliaries, appears.

Temperance, or agreement, is the virtue which relates to all classes.

Finally, there comes justice. "Justice is the ultimate cause and condition of all of them. . . . If a question should arise as to which of these four qualities contributed most by their presence to the excellence of the State whether the agreement of rulers and subjects or the preservation in the soldiers of the opinion which the law ordains about the true nature of dangers, or wisdom and watchfulness in the rulers would claim the palm, or whether this which I am about to mention," namely, "everyone doing his own work and not being a busybody—the question would not be easily determined." Nevertheless, it is plain that justice is the keystone of the Platonic utopia.

We must not misunderstand Plato's division of classes. Aristotle criticizes Plato in terms of a more simple system of democracy; but Plato did not mean to institute a fixed order; within his Republic the Napoleonic motto—*la carrière est ouverte aux talents*—was the guiding principle. What lay beneath Plato's argument was a belief which present-day studies in pyschology seem likely to confirm; a belief that children come into the world with a bent already well marked in their physical and mental constitutions. Plato advocated, it is true, an aristocracy or government by the best people; but he did not believe in fake aristocracies that are perpetuated through hereditary wealth and position. Having determined that his city was to contain three classes, rulers, warriors, and workers, his capital difficulty still remained to be faced; how was each individual to find his way to the right class,

[43]

and under what conditions would he best fulfill his functions there?

The answers to these questions bring us to the boldest and most original sections of the Republic: the part that has provoked the greatest amount of antagonism and aversion, because of its drastic departure from the rut of many established institutions—in particular, individual marriages and individual property.

In order to perpetuate his ideal constitution Plato relies upon three methods: breeding, education, and a discipline for the daily life. Let us consider the effect of these methods upon each of the classes.

We may dismiss the class of artisans and husbandmen very briefly. It is not quite clear whether Plato meant his system of marriage to extend to the members of this class. As for education, it is clear that he saw nothing to find fault with in the system of apprenticeship whereby the smith or the potter or the farmer trained others to follow his calling; and so he had no reason for departing from methods which had proved, on the whole, very satisfactory. How satisfactory that system was, indeed, we have only to look at an Athenian ruin or vase or chalice to find out. Any improvements that might come about in these occupations would result from the Platonic rule of justice; and Plato followed his own injunction strictly enough to keep away from other people's business.

This of course seems an odd and hasty manner of treatment, as I said before, to those of us who live in a world where the affairs of industry and the tendencies of the labor movement are forever on the carpet. But Plato justifies his treatment by saying that "when shoemakers become bad, and are degenerate, and profess to

be shoemakers when they are not, no great mischief
happens to the state; but when the guardians of the
law and the State are not so in reality, but only in
appearance, you see how they entirely destroy the
whole constitution, if they alone shall have the privilege of an affluent and happy life." Hence Plato con-
centrates his attack upon the point of greatest danger:
while the shoemaker, as a rule, knows how to mind his
own business, the statesman is for the most part unaware of the essential business which he has to mind;
and tends to be negligent even when he has some dim
notion as to what it may be—being all too ready to
sacrifice it to golf or the favors of a beautiful woman.
As we saw in Plato's original description of the State,
the common folk would doubtless have a good many
of the joys and delights traditional in the Greek cities;
and doubtless, although Plato says nothing one way or
the other, they would be permitted to own such property as might be needed for the conduct of their business
or the enjoyment of their homes. The very fact that
no definite rule was prescribed for them, makes us
suspect that Plato was willing to let these things go
on in the usual way.

The next class is known as the warriors, or auxiliaries. They are different in character from the
guardians who rule the state; but frequently Plato
refers to the guardians as a single class, including the
auxiliaries; and it seems that they figured in his
mind as the temporal arm of that class. At any
rate, the auxiliaries as they are painted in the Critias,
which was the dialogue in which Plato attempted to
show his Republic in action, dwelt by themselves within
a single enclosure; and had common meals and com-

mon temples of their own; and so we may surmise that their way of life was to be similar to that of the higher guardians, but that it was not capable of being pushed to the same pitch of development on the intellectual side. These warriors of Plato are, after all, not so very much unlike the regular or standing army in a modern State: they have a life of their own within the barracks, they are trained and drilled to great endurance, and they are taught to obey without question the Government. When you examine the naked business of the warriors and artisans, you discover that Plato is not, for all the difference in scale, so very far away from modern realities. Apart from the fact that women were permitted an equal place with men in the life of the camp and the gymnasium and the academy, the real difference comes in the matter of breeding and selection. At last we approach the Governors, or the Guardians.

How does the Guardian achieve his position and power? Plato is a little chary of answering this question; he hints that it can only happen at the beginning if a person with the brains of a philosopher happen to be born with the authority of a king. Let us pass this by. How are the Guardians born and bred? This is the manner.

For the well-being of the state the Guardians have the power to administer medicinal lies. One of these is to be told to the youth when their education has reached a point at which it becomes possible for the Guardians to determine their natural talents and aptitudes.

"Citizens, we shall say to them in our tale, you are brothers, yet God has framed you differently. Some of you have the power to command, and these he has composed of gold, wherefore also they have the greatest honor; others of silver, to be auxiliaries; others again who are to be husbandmen and craftsmen he has made of brass and iron; and the species will generally be preserved in the children. But as you are of the same original family, a golden parent will sometimes have a silver son, or a silver parent a golden son. And God proclaims to the rulers, as a first principle, that before all things they should watch over their offspring, and see what elements mingle in their nature, for if the son of a golden or silver parent has an admixture of brass and iron, then nature orders a transposition of the ranks; and the eye of the ruler must not be pitiful towards his child because he has to descend in the scale and will become a husbandman or artisan, just as there may be others sprung from the artisan class who are raised to honor, and become guardians and auxiliaries."

As the safeguard of this principle of natural selection of functions, Plato proposed a system of common marriage. "The wives of these guardians are to be common, and their children are also common, and no parent is to know his own child, nor any child his parent." Starting from the day of the hymeneal, the bridegroom who was then married will call all the male children who are born ten and seven months afterwards his sons, and the female children his daughters, and they will call him father. . . . And those who were born at the same time they will term brothers and sisters, and they are not to intermarry." One of the features of this system is that the best stocks—the strongest and wisest and most beautiful—are to be encouraged to reproduce themselves. But this is not worked out in detail. There is to be complete freedom of sexual selection among the guardians; and those who are most distinguished in their services are to have access to a great number of women; but beyond encouraging the guardians to be prolific, Plato did not apparently consider the possibilities of cross-breeding between the various classes.

On the whole, one may say that Plato puts it up to the Guardians to perpetuate themselves properly, and indicates that this is to be one of their main concerns. His good breeding was biological breeding, not social breeding. He recognized—as some of our modern eugenists have failed to—that good parents might throw poor stock, on occasion, and that abject parents might have remarkably good progeny. Even if the Guardians are to be encouraged to have good children, Plato provides that the children themselves must prove their goodness before they are in turn recognized as Guardians. As for the children of the baser sort—well, they were to be rigorously limited to the needs and resources of the community. Plato lived at a time when a great many children were born only to be murdered through "exposure" as it was called; and he had no qualms, apparently, about letting the Guardians send the children with a bad heredity into the discard. If his population could not grow properly in the sunlight without getting rid of the weeds, he was prepared to get rid of the weeds. People who were physically or spiritually too deformed to take part in the good life were to be eliminated. Plato, like a robust Athenian, was for killing or curing a disease; and he gave short shrift to the constitutional invalids.

[48]

But to breed Guardians is only one-half the problem. The other half comes under the heads of education and discipline; and when Plato discusses these things, he is not speaking, as a modern college president perhaps would, of book-learning alone; he is referring to all the activities that mold a person's life. He follows the older philosopher, Pythagoras, and anticipates the great organizer, Benedict, by laying down a rule of life for his guardians. He did not imagine that disinterested activities, spacious thoughts, and clear vision would arise in people who normally put their personal comfort and "happiness" above the necessities of their office.

Let us recognize the depth of Plato's insight. It is plain that he did not despise what a modern psychologist would call "the normal biological career." For the great majority of people happiness consisted in learning a definite trade or profession, in doing one's daily work, in mating, and when the tension of the day relaxed, in getting enjoyment and recreation in the simple sensualities of eating, drinking, singing, love-making, and what not. This normal biological career is associated with a home, and with the limited horizons of a home; and a host of small loyalties and jealousies and interests are woven into the very texture of that life.

Each home, each small circle of relatives and friends, tends to be a minature utopia; there is a limited community of goods, a tendency to adjust one's actions to the welfare of the little whole, and a habit of banding together against the world at large. But the good,

[49]

contrary to the proverb, is frequently the enemy of the better; and the little utopia of the family is the enemy—indeed the principal enemy—of the beloved community. This fact is notorious. The picture of a trade union leader which Mr. John Galsworthy portrays in Strife, whose power to act firmly in behalf of his group is sapped by the demands made by family ties, could be matched in a thousand places. In order to have the freedom to act for the sake of a great institution, a person must be stript of a whole host of restraining ties and sentimentalities. Jesus commanded his followers to leave their families and abandon their worldly goods; and Plato, in order to preserve his ideal commonwealth, laid down a similar rule. For those who as guardians were to apply the science of government to public affairs, a private life, private duties, private interests, were all to be left behind.

As to the education of the Guardians, I have scarcely the space to treat the more formal part of it in detail; for among other things, as Jowett points out, the Republic is a treatise on education; and Plato presents a fairly elaborate plan. The two branches of Greek education, music and gymnastic, applied in the student's early years to the culture of the body and the culture of the mind; and both branches were to be followed in common by both sexes. Instruction during the early part of a child's life was to be communicated through play activities, as it is today in the City and Country School in New York; and only with manhood did the student approach his subjects in a more formal and systematic manner. In the course of this education the students were to be tested again and again with respect to their mental keenness and tenacity and fortitude;

[50]

and only those who came through the fire purified and strengthened were to be admitted to the class of guardians.

The daily life of the Guardians is a rigorous, military regime. They live in common barracks, and in order to avoid paying attention to private affairs, instead of minding the good of the whole community, no one is allowed to "possess any substance privately, unless there be a great necessity for it"; next, Plato continues, none shall have any dwelling or storehouse into which whoever inclines may not enter; and as for necessaries, they shall be only such as brave and temperate warriors may require, and as they are supported by other citizens, they shall receive such a reward of their guardianship as to have neither an overplus nor a deficit at the end of the year. They shall have public meals, as in encampments, and live in common. They are to refrain from using gold and silver, as all the gold and silver they require is in their souls.

All these regulations, of course, are for the purpose of keeping the Guardians disinterested. Plato believed that the majority of people did not know how to mind public business; for it seemed to him that the ordering of a community's life required a measure of science which the common man could not possibly possess. Indeed, in a city of a thousand men he did not see the possibility of getting as many as fifty men who would be sufficiently well versed in what we should today call sociology to deal intelligently with public affairs—for there would scarcely be that many first-rate draughts players. At the same time, if the government is to be entrusted to a few, the few must be genuinely disinterested. If they possessed lands and houses and money

in a private way they would become landlords and
farmers instead of Guardians; they would be hateful
masters instead of allies of the citizens; and so "hating
and being hated, plotting and being plotted against,
more afraid of the enemies within than the enemies
without, they would drag themselves and the rest of the
state to speedy destruction."

It remains to take a glance at the manhood and
later life of the Guardians.

As young men, the Guardians belong to the auxiliaries; and since they are not permitted to perform any
of the manual arts—for skill in any of the trades tended
to make a man warped and one-sided, like the symbolic
blacksmith god, Hephæstos—their physical edge was
maintained by the unceasing discipline of the gymnasium and "military" expeditions. I put military in
quotation marks, because a greater part of the warriors' time is spent not in war but in preparation for
war; and it is plain that Plato looked upon war as an
unnecessary evil, for it arose out of the unjust state;
and therefore he must have resorted to warlike discipline
for the educational values he found in it. From thirty-
five to fifty the potential Guardians undertake practical
activities, commanding armies and gaining experience
of life. After fifty, those who are qualified devote themselves to philosophy: out of their experience and their
inner reflection they figure the essential nature of the
good community; and on occasion each guardian
abandons divine philosophy for a while, takes his turn
at the helm of the state, and trains his successors.

10

What is the business of the Guardian? How does

Plato's ideal statesman differ from Julius Cæsar or Mr. Theodore Roosevelt?

The business of the Guardian is to manufacture liberty. The petty laws, regulations, and reforms with which the ordinary statesman occupies himself had nothing to do, in Plato's mind, with the essential business of the ruler. So Plato expressly foregoes making laws to regulate marketing, the affairs of industry, graft, bribery, theft, and so forth; and he leaves these matters with the curt indication that men can be left to themselves to devise on a voluntary basis the rules of the game for the different occupations; and that it is not the business of the Guardian to meddle in such matters. In a well-founded state, a great number of minor maladjustments would simply fall out of existence; whilst in any other state, all the tinkering and reforming in the world is quite powerless to amend its organic defects. Those make-believe statesmen who try their hand at legislation and "are always fancying that by reforming they will make an end of the dishonesties and rascalities of mankind," do not know that in reality they are trying to cut away the heads of a hydra.

The real concern of the Guardians is with the essential constitution of the state. The means that they employ to perfect this constitution are breeding, vocational selection, and education. "If once a republic is set a-going, it proceeds happily, increasing as a circle. And whilst good education and nurture are preserved, they produce good geniuses; and good geniuses, partaking of such education, produce still better than the former, as well in other respects, as with reference to propagation, as in the case of other animals." All the activities of the Republic are to be patterned after the utopia which the Guardians see with their inward eye. So gradually the community becomes a living unity; and it exhibits the health of that which is organically sound.

11

What do we miss when we look around this utopia of Plato's? Contacts with the outside world? We may take them for granted. Downy beds, Corinthian girls, luxurious furniture? We can well spare them. The opportunity for a satisfactory intellectual and physical life? No: both of these are here.

What Plato has left out are the poets, dramatists, and painters. Literature and music, in order to contribute to the noble education of the Guardians, are both severely restricted in theme and in treatment. Plato has his limitations; and here is the principal one: Plato distrusted the emotional life, and whilst he was prepared to do full homage to man's obvious sensualities, he feared the emotions as a tight-rope walker fears the wind; for they threatened his balance. In one significant passage he classifies "love" with disease and drunkenness, as a vulgar misfortune; and though he was ready to permit the active expression of the emotions, as in the dance or the sexual act, he treated the mere play upon the feelings, without active participation, as a form of intemperance. Hence a great deal of music and dramatic mimicry was taboo. Foreign as this doctrine sounds to the modern reader, there is perhaps more than a grain of sense in it: William James used to teach that no one should passively experience an emotion at a concert or a play without trying to express that emotion actively as soon as he could make the opportunity. At any rate, let us leave this problem which Plato opens up with a free mind; and note here in passing that in the utopia of William Morris novels drop naturally out of existence because life is too active an ectasy to be fed with the pathetic, the maudlin, and the diseased.

12

As we leave this little city of Plato's, nestling in the hills, and as the thin, didactic voice of Plato, who has been perpetually at our elbows, dies away from our ears—what impression do we finally carry away?

In the fields, men are perhaps plowing the land for the autumn sowing; on the terraces, a band of men, women, and children are plucking the olives carefully from the trees, one by one; in the gymnasium on the top of the Acropolis, men and youths are exercising, and as they practice with the javelin now and then it catches the sun and glints into our eye; apart from these groups, in a shaded walk that overlooks the city, a Guardian is pacing back and forth, talking in quick, earnest tones with his pupils.

These are occupations which, crudely or elaborately, men have always engaged in; and here in the Republic they engage in them still. What has changed? What has profoundly changed is not the things that men do, but the relations they bear to one another in doing them. In Plato's community, servitude and compulsion and avarice and indolence are gone. Men mind their business for the sake of living well, in just relations to the whole community of which they are a part. They live, in the strictest sense, according to nature; and because no one can enjoy a private privilege, each man can grow to his full stature and enter into every heritage of his citizenship. When Plato says no to the institutions and ways of life that men have blindly fostered, his eyes are open, and he is facing the light.

CHAPTER THREE

How something happened to utopia between Plato and
Sir Thomas More; and how utopia was discovered
again, along with the New World.

CHAPTER THREE

1

THERE is a span of nearly two thousand years between Plato and Sir Thomas More. During that time, in the Western World at any rate, utopia seems to disappear beyond the horizon. Plutarch's Life of Lycurgus looks back into a mythical past; Cicero's essay on the state is a negligible work; and St. Augustine's City of God is chiefly remarkable for a brilliant journalistic attack upon the old order of Rome which reminds one of the contemporary diatribes of Maximilian Harden. Except for these works there is, as far as I can discover, scarcely any other piece of writing which even hints at utopia except as utopia may refer to a dim golden age in the past when all men were virtuous and happy.

But while utopia dropt out of literature, it did not drop out of men's minds; and the utopia of the first fifteen hundred years after Christ is transplanted to the sky, and called the Kingdom of Heaven. It is distinctly a utopia of escape. The world as men find it is full of sin and trouble. Nothing can be done about it except to repent of the sin and find refuge from the trouble in the life after the grave. So the utopia of Christianity is fixed and settled: one can enter into the Kingdom of Heaven if a passport has been granted, but one can do nothing to create or mold this heaven. Change and struggle and ambition and amelioration

[59]

belong to the wicked world, and bring no final satisfaction. Happiness lies not in the deed, but in having
a secure credit in the final balance of accounts—happiness, in other words, lies in the ultimate compensation.
This world of fading empires and dilapidated cities
is no home except for the violent and the "worldly."

If the idea of utopia loses its practical hold during
this period, the will-to-utopia remains; and the rise of
the monastic system and the attempts of the great popes
from Hildebrand onward to establish a universal empire under the shield of the church show that, as always,
there was a breach between the ideas which people carried in their heads and the things which actual circumstances and going institutions compelled them to do.
There is no need to consider these partial, institutional
utopias until we get down to the nineteenth century.
What concerns us now is that the Kingdom of Heaven,
as a utopia of escape, ceased to hold men's allegiance
when they discovered other channels and other possibilities.

The shift from a heavenly utopia to a worldly one
came during that period of change and uneasiness which
characterized the decline of the Middle Age. Its first
expression is the "Utopia" of Sir Thomas More, the
great chancellor who served under Henry VIII.

2

In the introduction to More's "Utopia" one gets a
vivid impression of the forces that were stirring men's
minds out of the sluggish routine into which they had
settled. The man who is supposed to describe the
commonwealth of Utopia is a Portuguese scholar,

[60]

learned in Greek. He has left his family possessions with his kinsmen and has gone adventuring for other continents with Americus Vesputius. This Raphael Hythloday is the sort of sunburnt sailor one could probably have encountered in Bristol or Cadiz or Antwerp almost any day during the late part of the fifteenth century. He has abandoned Aristotle, whom the schoolmen had butchered and had made pemmican of, and through his conquest of Greek he has come into possession of that new learning which stems back to Plato; and his brain is teeming with the criticisms and suggestions of a strange, pagan philosophy. Moreover, he has been abroad to the Americas or the Indies, and he is ready to tell all who will listen of a strange land on the other side of the world, where, as Sterne said of France, "they do things better." No institution is too fantastic but that it might exist—on the other side of the world. No way of life is too reasonable but that a philosophical population might follow it—on the other side of the world. Conceive of the world of ideas which Greek literature had just opened up coming headlong against the new lands which the magnetic compass had given men the courage to explore, and utopia, as a fresh conception of the good life, becomes a throbbing possibility.

3

In setting out for Utopia Sir Thomas More left behind a scene which in its political violence and economic maladjustment looks queerly like our own. Indeed, there are a good many passages which need only have a few names altered and the language itself cast into modern English in order to serve as editorial comment for a radical weekly review.

Consider this man Raphael Hythloday, this errant member of the intelligentzia. Life as he knows it in the Europe of his day no longer has a hold upon him. The rich are fattening upon the poor; land is being gathered into big parcels, at least in England; and turned over into sheep runs. The people who used to cultivate the land are compelled to leave their few acres and are thrown on their own resources. Soldiers who have returned from the wars can find nothing to do; disabled veterans and people accustomed to live as pensioners on the more prosperous have become destitute. Extravagant luxury grows on one hand; misery on the other. Those who are poor, beg; those who are proud, steal; and for their pains the thieves and the vagrants are tried and sentenced to the gibbet, where by dozens they hang before the eyes of the market crowds.

Just as today, people complain that the laws are not strict enough or that they are not enforced; and everyone stubbornly refuses to look at the matter through Raphael Hythloday's eyes and to see that the robbery and violence which are abroad are not a cause of bad times but a result of them.

What can a man of intelligence do in such a world?

More's friend, Peter Giles, who is represented as the sponsor for Raphael, wonders why a man of Raphael's talent does not enter into the service of the king— in short, go in for politics. Raphael answers that he does not wish to be enslaved; and he cannot try to fetch happiness on terms so abhorrent to his disposition, for "most princes apply themselves more to the affairs of war than to the useful arts of peace, and are more set on acquiring new kingdoms right or wrong than on governing those they possess." There is no use trying to tell them about the wiser institutions of the Utopians: if they could not refute your arguments they would say that the old ways were good enough for their ancestors and are good enough for them, even though they have willingly let go of all the genuinely good things that might have been inherited from the past.

So much for the help an intelligent man might give on domestic problems. As for international affairs, it is a mess of chicane and intrigue and brigandage. While so many people of influence are advising preparedness and "how to carry on the war," what chance would a poor intellectual like Hythloday have if he stood up and said that the government should withdraw their armies from foreign parts and try to improve conditions at home, instead of oppressing the people with taxes and spilling their blood without bringing them a single blessed advantage, whilst their manners are being corrupted by a long war, and their laws fall into contempt, with robbery and murder on every hand.

More, through the tongue of Raphael Hythloday, is painting a picture of the life he sees about him; but in it we seem to see every feature of our own national countenance.

This unhonored and disoriented intellectual is the very emblem of some of our best spirits today. Rack and ruin have gone too far to admit of any sort of repair except that which proceeds from the bottom up; and so Hythloday freely admits that "as long as there is any property, and while money is the standard of all other things, I cannot think that a nation can be governed either justly or happily; not justly, because

[63]

the best things will fall to the share of the worst men; nor happily, because all things will be divided among a few (and even these are not in all respects happy), the rest being left to be absolutely miserable." In short, says Hythloday, there is no salvation except through following the practices of the Utopians.

So the new world of exploration brings us within sight of a new world of ideas, and the beloved community, whose seed Plato had sought to implant in men's minds, springs up again, after a fallow period of almost two thousand years. What sort of country is it?

4

Geographically viewed, the island of Utopia exists only in More's imagination. All that we can say of it is that it is two hundred miles broad, shaped something like a crescent, with an entrance into its great bay which lends itself to defence. There are fifty-four cities in the island; the nearest is twenty-four miles from its neighbor, and the farthest is not more than a day's march distant. The chief town, Amaurot, is situated very nearly in the center; and each city has jurisdiction over the land for twenty miles around; so that here again we find the city-region as the unit of political life.

5

The economic base of this commonwealth is agriculture, and no one is ignorant of the art. Here and there over the countryside are great farm-houses, equipt for carrying on agricultural operations. While those who are well-adapted for rural life are free to live in the

[64]

open country the whole year round, other workers are sent by turns from the city to take part in the farm-labor. Every farmstead or "family" holds no less than forty men and women. Each year twenty of this family come back to town after two years in the country; and in their place another twenty is sent out from the town, so that they may learn the country work from those who have had at least a year's experience.

Agricultural economics is so well advanced that the countryside knows exactly how much food is needed by the whole city-region; but the Utopians sow and breed more abundantly than they need, in order that their neighbors may have the overplus. Poultry-raising is also highly advanced. The Utopians "breed an infinite multitude of chickens in a very curious manner; for the hens do not sit and hatch them, but vast num-bers of eggs are laid in a gentle and equal heat, in order to be hatched"—in short, they have discovered the incubator!

During the harvest season the country magistrates inform the city magistrates how many extra hands are needed for reaping; a draft of city workers is made, and the work is commonly done in short order.

While every man, woman, and child knows how to cultivate the soil, since each has learned partly in school and partly by practice, every person also has some "peculiar trade to which he applies himself, such as the manufacture of wool or flax, masonry, smith's work or carpenter's work"; and no trade is held in special esteem above the others. (That is a great jump from the Republic where the mechanic arts are con-sidered base and servile in nature!) The same trade usually passes down from father to son, since each

[65]

family follows its own special occupation; but a man whose genius lies another way may be adopted into a family which plies another trade; and if after he has learnt that trade, he wishes still to master another, this change is brought about in the same manner. "When he has learned both, he follows that which he likes best, unless the public has more occasion for the other."

The chief and almost the only business of the magistrates is to see that no one lives in idleness. This does not mean that the Utopians wear themselves out with "perpetual toil from morning to night, as if they were beasts of burden," for they appoint eight hours for sleep and six for work, and the rest of the day is left to each man's discretion. They are able to cut down the length of time needed for work, without our so-called labor saving machinery, by using the services of classes which in More's time were given for the most part to idleness—princes, rich men, healthy beggars, and the like. The only exception to this rule of labor is with the magistrates—who are not in the habit of taking advantage of it—and the students, who upon proving their ability are released from mechanical operations. If there is too great a surplus of labor, men are sent out to repair the highways; but when no public undertaking is to be performed, the hours of work are lessened.

6

So much for the daily industrial life of the Utopians. How are the goods distributed?

Between the city and the country there is a monthly exchange of goods. This occasion is made a festival,

[66]

and the country people come into town and take back
for themselves the goods which the townspeople have
made; and the magistrates "take care to see it given
to them." In back of this direct interchange of goods
between town and country, between household and
household, there are doubtless regulations; and it is
simply our misfortune that Raphael Hythloday did not
think it necessary to go into them. Within the cities,
we must add, there are storehouses where a daily market
takes place.

As with the business of production, the family is the
unit of distribution; and the city is composed of these
units, rather than of a multitude of isolated individuals.
"Every city is divided into four equal parts, and in the
middle of each there is a market-place; what is brought
hither, and manufactured by the several families, is
carried from thence to houses appointed for that purpose, in which all things of a sort are laid by themselves;
and thither every father goes and takes whatever he
or his family stand in need of, without either paying
for it or leaving anything in exchange. There is no
reason for giving denial to any person, since there is
such plenty of everything among them; and there is no
danger of a man's asking for more than he needs; they
have no inducements to do this, since they are sure
they shall always be supplied."

More goes on to explain this direct system of exchange, and to justify it. "It is the fear of want that
makes any of the whole race of animals either greedy
or ravenous, but besides fear, there is in man a pride
that makes him fancy it a particular glory to excel
others in pomp and excess. But by the laws of the
Utopians there is no room for this. Near these mar-

[67]

kets are others for all sorts of provisions, where there are not only herbs, fruits, and bread, but also fish, fowl, and cattle. There are also, without their towns, places appointed near some running water for killing their beasts, and for washing away their filth."

In addition to the monthly apportionment of goods by the local magistrates, the great council which meets at Amaurot once a year undertakes to examine the production of each region, and those regions that suffer from a scarcity of goods are supplied out of the surplus of other regions, "so that indeed the whole island is, as it were, one family."

Taking it all together, there is pretty much the same standard of well-being that we found in the Republic. More recognizes the instinct for self-assertion and the exhibitionist element in man's makeup; but he does not pander to it. The precious metals are held in contempt: gold is used to make chamberpots and chains for slaves; pearls are given to children who glory in them and enjoy them while they are young and are as much ashamed to use them afterwards as they are of their puppets and other toys. Gaudy clothes and jewelry are likewise out of fashion in Utopia. The shopkeepers of Bond Street and Fifth Avenue would break their hearts here; for it is impossible to spend money or to spend other people's labor on articles which lend themselves solely to conspicuous display, and are otherwise neither useful nor beautiful. Contrast More's Utopia with St. John's vision of heaven, and the worldly Utopia seems quite naked and austere. Two hundred years later, in Penn's city of Philadelphia, we might have fancied that we were walking about the streets of Amaurot.

[68]

7

The town life of the Utopians, as I have explained, rests upon rural foundations; there is such a mixture of town and country as Peter Kropotkin sought to realize in his sketch of "Fields, Factories, and Workshops." Let us conjure up the town of Amaurot and see in what sort of environment the townspeople spend their days. Our Utopian city, alas! reminds us somewhat of its rivals in latter-day America; for Raphael tells us that he who knows one of their towns knows all of them.

Amaurot lies on the side of a hill; it is almost a square, two miles on each side; and it faces the river Anider which takes its rise eighty miles above the town, and gets lost in the ocean sixty miles below. The town is compassed by a high, thick wall; the streets are convenient for carriages and sheltered from the winds; and the houses are built in rows so that a whole side of the street looks like a single unit. (It was so that the great people built their houses in eighteenth century London and Edinburgh, as Belgrave Square, Charlotte Square, and the great Adelphi Mansion designed by the Brothers Adam show us.) The streets are twenty feet broad; and in back of the houses are gardens, which everyone has a hand in keeping up; and the people of the various blocks vie with each other in ordering their gardens, so that there is "nothing belonging to the whole town that is more useful and more pleasant."

In every street there are great halls, distinguished by particular names, and lying at an equal distance from each other. In each hall dwells the magistrates of a district, who rules over thirty families, fifteen living on one side and fifteen on another; and since a family consists of not more than sixteen and not less than ten people, this magistrate—or Philarch as he is called —is the "community leader" of some four hundred people.

In these halls everyone meets and takes his principal meal. The stewards go to the market place at a particular hour, and, according to the number of people in their halls, carry home provisions. The people who are in hospitals—which are built outside the walls and are so large they might pass for little towns—get the pick of the day's food. At the hours of dinner and supper the whole block is called together by a trumpet, and everybody joins company, except such as are sick or in hospital, just as the students and fellows to this day eat their principal meal in an Oxford college. The dressing of meat and the ordering of the tables belongs to the women; all those of every family taking their place by turns. In the same building there is a common nursery and chapel; and so the women who have children to care for labor under no inconvenience.

The midday meal is dispatched unceremoniously; but at the end of the day music always accompanies the meals, perfumes are burnt or sprinkled around, and they "want nothing that may cheer up their spirits." Bond Street and Fifth Avenue may weep about the absence of conspicuous waste in Utopia; but at supper time, at any rate, William Penn would be uncomfortable. There is the odor of an uncommonly good club in the description of the final meal of the day: the smell of the barracks or the poorhouse, which we should find later in Robert Owen's common halls, does not intrude for an instant. More, when you examine him closely, does not altogether forget the mean sensual man who dwells occasionally in all of us!

8

Now that we have laid the foundations of the material life, we must observe the limitations that are laid upon the daily activities of the Utopians. This brings us to the government.

The basis of the Utopian political state, as in the economic province, is the family. Every year thirty families choose a magistrate, known as a Philarch; and over every ten Philarchs, with the families subject to them, there is an Archphilarch. All the Philarchs, who are in number 200, choose the Prince out of a list of four, who are named by the people of the four divisions of the city. The Prince is elected for life, unless he be removed on suspicion of attempting to enslave the people. The Philarchs are chosen for a single year; but they are frequently re-elected. In order to keep their rulers from conspiring to upset the government, no matter of great importance can be set on foot without being sent to the Philarchs, "who, after they have communicated it to the families that belong to their divisions, and have considered it among themselves, make report to the senate; and upon great occasions the matter is referred to the council of the whole island."

Recollect that each household is an industrial as well as a domestic unit, as was usual in the Middle Age, and you will perceive that this is an astute combination of industrial and political democracy on a genuine basis of common interest.

[71]

The greater part of the business of the government relates to the economic life of the people. There are certain other matters, however, which remain over for them; and these affairs constitute a blot on More's conception of the ideal commonwealth. One of them is the regulation of travel; another is the treatment of crime; and a third is war.

It is interesting to note that on two subjects which More is mightily concerned to rectify in his own country—crime and war—he establishes conditions which are pretty far from being ideal or humane in his Utopia. A. E. has well said that a man becomes the image of the thing he hates. Everything that Raphael brings up against the government of England in the Introduction to Utopia could be brought with almost equal force, I believe, against the very country which is to serve as a standard.

While any man may travel if there is no particular occasion for him at home—whether he wishes to visit friends or see the rest of the country—it is necessary for him to carry a passport from the Prince. If he stay in any place longer than a night he must follow his proper occupation; and if anyone goes out of the city without leave or is found wandering around without a passport, he is punished as a fugitive, and upon committing the offense a second time is condemned to slavery. This is a plain example of unimaginative harshness; and it is hard to explain away; indeed, I have no intention to.

Apparently More could not conceive of a perfectly happy commonwealth for the majority of men if they still had to perform certain filthy daily tasks, like the slaughtering of beef; and so he attempts to kill two

[72]

birds with one stone: he creates a class of slaves, and
he fills this class by condemning to it people who have
committed venial crimes. In doing this, he overlooks
the final objection to slavery in all its forms; namely,
that it tends to corrupt the master.

Since we are discussing the conditions that undermine More's commonwealth, we may remark that war,
too, remains; the difference being that the Utopians
attempt to do by strategy, corruption, and what we
should now call propaganda what less intelligent people
do by sheer force of arms. If the Utopian incubator
anticipates the modern invention, their method of con-
ducting war likewise anticipates our modern technique
of undermining the enemy's morale: these Utopians, in
the good and the bad, are our contemporaries! Among
the just causes of war the Utopians count the seizure
of territory, the oppression of foreign merchants, and
the denial of access to land to nations capable of culti-
vating it. They take considerable pains to keep their
"best sort of men for their own use at home, so they
make use of the worst sort of men for the consumption
of war." In other words, they regard war as a means,
among other things, of weeding out undesirable elements
in the community.

It is a relief to turn away from these residual
iniquities to marriage and religion!

In marriage there is a curious mixture of the personal conception of sexual relations, which is the
modern note, with a belief in certain formal specifications which was the distinctly mediæval quality. Thus
on one hand the Utopians take care that the bride and
the bridegroom are introduced to each other, in their
nakedness, before the ceremony; and the grounds for

divorce are adultery and insufferable perverseness. When two people cannot agree they are permitted to escape the bond by mutual agreement under approval granted by the Senate after strict inquiry. On the other hand, unchastity is sternly punished, and those who commit adultery are condemned to slavery and not given the privilege of a second marriage.

In religion there is complete toleration for all creeds, with this exception: that those who dispute violently about religion or attempt to use any other force than that of mild persuasion are punished for breaking the public peace.

9

There is not the space to follow the life of the Utopians in all its details. It is time to discuss the world of ideas by which these Utopians chart their daily activities. This exposition of the basic Utopian values has been so admirably put by Sir Thomas More himself that the greater part of our conclusion will inevitably fall within quotation marks.

The Utopians "define virtue thus: that it is a living according to Nature, and think that we are made by God for that end; they believe that a man then follows Nature when he pursues or avoids things according to the direction of reason. . . . Reason directs us to keep our minds as free from passion and as cheerful as we can, and that we should consider ourselves bound by the ties of good-nature and humanity to use our utmost endeavors to help forward the happiness of all other persons; for there never was any man such a morose and severe pursuer of virtue, such an enemy to pleasure, that though he set hard rules for men

[74]

to undergo much pain, many watchings and other rigors, yet did not at the same time advise them to do all they could to relieve and ease the miserable, and who did not represent gentleness and good nature as amiable dispositions. . . . A life of pleasure is either a real evil, and in that case we ought not to assist others in their pursuit of it, but, on the contrary, to keep them from it all we can, as from that which is most hurtful and deadly; or if it is a good thing, so that we not only may but ought to help others to it, why then ought not a man to begin with himself? Since no man can be more bound to look after the good of another than after his own. . . .

"Thus as they define Virtue to be living according to Nature, so they imagine that Nature prompts all people to seek after pleasure, as the end of all they do. They also observe that in order to further our supporting the pleasures of life, Nature inclines us to enter into society; for there is no man so much raised above the rest of mankind as to be the only favorite of Nature, who, on the contrary, seems to have placed on a level all those that belong to the same species. Upon this they infer that no man ought to seek his own conveniences so eagerly as to prejudice others; and therefore they think that all agreements between private persons ought to be observed, but likewise that all those laws ought to be kept, which either a good prince has published in due form, to which a people that is neither oppressed with tyranny nor circumvented by fraud, has consented, for distributing these conveniences of life which afford us all our pleasures.

"They think it is an evidence of true wisdom for a man to pursue his own advantages, as far as the laws allow it. They account it piety to prefer public good to one's private concerns; but they think it unjust for a man to seek for pleasure by snatching another man's pleasures from him.

"Thus upon an inquiry into the whole matter, they reckon that all our actions, and even all our virtues, terminate in pleasure, as in our chief end and greatest happiness; and they call every motion or state, either of body or mind, in which Nature teaches us to delight, a pleasure. They cautiously limit pleasure only to those appetites to which Nature leads us; for they say that Nature leads us only to those delights to which reason as well as sense carries us, and by which we neither injure any other person nor lose the possession of greater pleasures, and of such as draw no troubles after them."

Thus the Utopians discriminate between natural pleasures and those which have some sting or bitterness concealed in them. The love of fine clothes is considered by Utopians as a pleasure of the latter sort; likewise is the desire of those who possess fine clothes to be kowtowed to by other people. Men who heap up wealth without using it are in the same class; and those who throw dice or hunt—for in Utopia hunting is turned over to the butchers, and the butchers are slaves.

Now Utopians "reckon up several sorts of pleasures which they call true ones; some belong to the body and others to the mind. The pleasures of the mind lie in knowledge, and in that delight which the contemplation of truth carries with it; to which they add the joyful reflections on a well-spent life; and the assured hopes of a future happiness. They divide the pleasures of

[76]

the body into two sorts; the one is that which gives our
senses some real delight, and is performed, either by
recruiting nature, and supplying those parts which
feed the internal heat of life by eating and drinking;
or when nature is eased of any surcharge that oppresses
it; when we are relieved from sudden pain, or that which
arises from satisfying the appetite which Nature has
wisely given for the propagation of the species. There
is another kind of pleasure that arises neither from our
receiving what the body requires, nor its being relieved
when overcharged, and yet by a secret, unseen virtue
affects the senses, raises the passions, and strikes the
mind with generous impressions; this is the pleasure
that arises from music. Another kind of bodily
pleasure is that which arises from an undisturbed and
vigorous constitution of body, when life and active
spirits seem to actuate every part. This lively health,
when entirely free from all mixture of pain, of itself
gives an inward pleasure . . . and Utopians reckon
it the foundation and basis of all the other joys of life,
since this alone makes the state of life easy and desirable; and when this is wanting a man is really capable
of no other pleasure." The crowning pleasure of the
Utopian is the cultivation of the mind; and the leisure
hours of the people, as well as the professional scholars,
are spent in the lecture hall and the study.

10

Such are the goals for which the Utopians direct
their social order. These values are, I need scarcely
point out, rooted in the nature of man, and not in any
set of external institutions. The aim of every Utopian

institution is to help every man to help himself. When we put the matter in these bald phrases, what More brings forward seems weak and platitudinous. Behind it all, however, is a vital idea: namely, that our attempts to live the good life are constantly perverted by our efforts to gain a living; and that by juggling gains and advantages, by striving after power and riches and distinction, we miss the opportunity to live as whole men. People become the nursemaids of their furniture, their property, their titles, their position; and so they lose the direct satisfaction that furniture or property would give.

To cultivate the soil rather than simply to get away with a job; to take food and drink rather than to earn money; to think and dream and invent, rather than to increase one's reputation; in short, to grasp the living reality and spurn the shadow—this is the substance of the Utopian way of life. Power and wealth and dignity and fame are abstractions; and men cannot live by abstractions alone. In this Utopia of the New World every man has the opportunity to be a man because no one else has the opportunity to be a monster. Here, too, the chief end of man is that he should grow to the fullest stature of his species.

CHAPTER FOUR

How the new Humanism of the Renascence brings us
within sight of Christianopolis; and how we have
for the first time a glimpse of a modern utopia.

CHAPTER FOUR

1

A HUNDRED years pass, and the man who next conducts us into Utopia is a Humanist scholar. After the manner of his time, he answers to the latinized name, Johann Valentin Andreæ. He is a traveller, a social reformer, and above all things a preacher; and so the vision he imparts to us of Christianopolis seems occasionally to flicker into blackness whilst he moralizes for us and tells us to the point of tedium what his views are concerning the life of man, and in particular the conceptions of Christianity which his countrymen, the Germans, are debating about. Sometimes, when we are on the point of coming to grips with his utopia, he will annoy us by going off on a long tirade about the wickedness of the world and the necessity for fastening one's gaze upon the life hereafter—for Protestantism seems just as other-worldly as Catholicism. It is the Humanist Andreæ rather than the Lutheran Andreæ who paints the picture of a Christian city. While Andreæ sticks to Christianopolis his insight is deep, his views are sound, and his proposals are rational; and more than once he will amaze us by putting forward ideas which seem to leap three hundred years ahead of his time and environment.

It is impossible to get rid of the personal flavor of Andreæ: his fine intelligence and his candor make our contacts with Christianopolis quite different from the dreary guidebook sketches which some of the later utopians will inflict upon us. The two other utopians who wrote in the same half century as Andreæ—Francis Bacon and Tommaso Campanella—are quite second-rate in comparison; Bacon with his positively nauseating foppishness about details in dress and his superstitious regard for forms and ceremonials, and Campanella, the lonely monk whose City of the Sun seems a marriage of Plato's Republic and the Court of Montezuma. When Bacon talks about science, he talks like a court costumer who is in the habit of describing the stage properties for a masque; and it is hard to tell whether he is more interested in the experiments performed by the scientists of the New Atlantis or the sort of clothes they wear while engaged in them. There is nothing of the snob or the dilettante about Andreæ: His eye fastens itself upon essentials, and he never leaves them except when—for he is necessarily a man of his age—he turns his gaze piously to heaven.

This teeming, struggling European world that Andreæ turns his back upon he knows quite well; for he has lived in Herrenburg, Koenigsbrunn, Tuebingen, Strassburg, Heidelberg, Frankfurt, Geneva, Vaihingen, and Calw; and he is in correspondence with learned men abroad, in particular with Samuel Hartlib, who lives in England, and with John Amos Comenius. Like the Chancellor in Christianopolis, he longs for an "abode situated below the sky, but at the same time above the dregs of this known world." Quite simply, he finds himself wrecked on the shore of an island dominated by the city of Christianopolis. After being examined as to his ideas of life and morals, his person, and his culture, he is admitted to the community.

2

This island is a whole world in miniature. As in the
Republic, the unit once more is the valley section, for
the "island is rich in grain and pasture fields, watered
with rivers and brooks, adorned with woods and vineyards, full of animals."

In outward appearance, Christianopolis does not
differ very much from the pictures of the cities one
finds in seventeenth century travel books, except for a
unity and orderliness that these cities sometimes lack.
"Its shape is a square whose side is 700 feet, well fortified with four towers and a wall. . . . It looks therefore towards the four quarters of the earth. Of buildings there are two rows, or if you count the seat of the
government and the storehouses, four; there is only one
public street, and only one marketplace, but this one is
of a very high order." In the middle of the city there
is a circular temple, a hundred feet in diameter; all the
buildings are three stories; and public balconies lead
to them. Provision against fire is made by building
the houses of burnt stone and separating them by fire-
proof walls. In general, "things look much the same
all around, not extravagant nor yet unclean; fresh air
and ventilation are provided throughout. About four
hundred citizens live here in religious faith and peace
of the highest order." The whole city is divided into
three parts, one to supply food, one for drill and exercise, and one for looks. The remainder of the island
serves the purposes of agriculture, and for workshops.

3

When we look back upon the Republic, with its external organization so plainly modeled upon military

Sparta, we see the camp and the soldier giving the pattern to the life of the whole community. In Utopia, the fundamental unit was the farmstead and the family; and family discipline, which arises naturally enough in rural conditions, was transferred to the city. In Christianopolis, the workshop and the worker set the lines upon which the community is developed; and whatever else this society may be, it is a "republic of workers, living in equality, desiring peace, and renouncing riches." If Utopia exhibits the communism of the family, Christianopolis presents the communism of the guild.

Industrially speaking, there are three sections in Christianopolis. One of them is devoted to agriculture and animal husbandry. Each of these departments has appropriate buildings, and directly opposite them is a rather large tower which connects them with the city buildings; under the tower a broad vaulted entrance leads into the city, and a smaller one to the individual houses. The dome of this tower roofs what we should call a guildhall, and here the citizens of the quarter come together as often as required to "act on sacred as well as civil matters." It is plain that these workers are not sheep led by wise shepherds, as in the Republic, but the members of autonomous, self-regulating groups.

The next quarter contains the mills, bake-shops, meat-shops, and factories for making whatever is done with machinery apart from fire. As Christianopolis welcomes originality in invention, there are a variety of enterprises within this domain; among them, paper manufacturing plants, saw mills, and establishments for grinding and polishing arms and tools. There are common kitchens and wash houses, too; for, as we shall

[84]

see presently, life in this ideal city corresponds to what we experience today in New York, London, and many another modern industrial city.

The third quarter is given over to the metallurgical industries, as well as to those like the glass, brick, and earthenware industries which require constant fire. It is necessary to point out that in planning the industrial quarters of Christianopolis, these seventeenth century Utopians have anticipated the best practice that has been worked out today, after a century of disorderly building. The separation of the city into zones, the distinction between "heavy" industries and "light" industries, the grouping of similar industrial establishments, the provision of an agricultural zone adjacent to the city—in all this our garden cities are but belated reproductions of Christianopolis.

Moreover, in Christianopolis, there is a conscious application of science to industrial processes; one might almost say that these artisans believed in efficiency engineering; for "here in truth you see a testing of nature herself. The men are not driven to a work with which they are unfamiliar, like pack-animals to their task, but they have been trained before in an accurate knowledge of scientific matters," on the theory that "unless you analyze matter by experiment, unless you improve the deficiencies of knowledge by more capable instruments, you are worthless." The dependence of industrial improvement upon deliberate scientific research may be a new discovery for the practical man, but it is an old story in Utopia.

4

What is the character of this artisan democracy?

[85]

The answer to this is summed up in one of those sayings that Andreæ, in the midst of his energetic exposition, drops by the way.

"To be wise and to work are not incompatible, if there is moderation."

So it follows that "their artisans are almost entirely educated men. For that which other people think is the proper characteristic of a few (and yet if you consider the stuffing of inexperience by learning, the characteristic of too many already) this, the inhabitants argue, should be attained by all individuals. They say that neither the substance of letters is such, nor yet the difficulty of work, that one man, if given enough time, cannot master both."

"Their work, or as they prefer to hear it called, 'the employment of their hands,' is conducted in a certain prescribed way, and all things are brought into a public booth. From here every workman receives out of the stock on hand whatever is necessary for the work of the coming week. For the whole city is, as it were, one single workshop, but of all different sorts and crafts. The ones in charge of these duties are stationed in the small towers at the corners of the wall; they know ahead of time what is to be made, in what quantity, and of what form, and they inform the mechanics of these items. If the supply of material in the work booth is sufficient, the workmen are permitted to indulge and give free play to their inventive genius. No one has any money, nor is there any use for any private money; yet the republic has its own treasury. And in this respect the inhabitants are especially blessed, because no one can be superior to the other in the amount of riches owned, since the advantage is rather one of power and genius, and the highest respect that of morals and piety. They have very few working hours, yet no less is accomplished than in other places, as it is considered disgraceful by all that one should take more rest and leisure time than is allowed."

In addition to the special trades, there are "public duties to which all citizens have obligation, such as watching, guarding, harvesting of grain and wine, working roads, erecting buildings, draining ground; also certain duties of assisting in the factories which are imposed upon all in turn according to age and sex, but not very often nor for a long time. For even though certain experienced men are put in charge of all the duties, yet when men are asked for, no one refuses the state his services and strength. For what we are in our homes, they are in their city, which they not undeservedly think a home. And for this reason it is no disgrace to perform any public function. . . . Hence all work, even that which is considered rather irksome, is accomplished in good time, and without much difficulty, since the promptness of the great number of workmen permits them easily to collect or distribute the great mass of things."

In this Christianopolis, as Mr. Bertrand Russell would put it, the creative rather than the possessive impulses are uppermost. Work is the main condition of existence, and this good community faces it. It is a pretty contrast to the attitude of the leisured classes who, as Andreæ says, with an entirely mistaken sense of delicacy shrink from touching earth, water, stones, coal, and things of that sort, but think it grand to have in their possession to delight them "horses, dogs, harlots and other similar creatures."

[87]

5

The place of commerce in this scheme of life is simple. It does not exist for the sake of individual gain. Hence no one engages in commerce on his own hook, for such matters are put in the hands of "those selected to attend to them," and the aim of commerce is not to gain money but to increase the variety of things at the disposal of the local community; so that—and again Andreæ steps in for emphasis—"we may see the peculiar production of each land, and so communicate with each other that we may seem to have the advantages of the universe in one place, as it were."

6

The constitution of the family in Christianopolis follows pretty definitely upon the lines dictated by urban occupations; for Andreæ is a city man, and since he does not despise the advantages city life can give, he does not shrink from their consequences. One of these consequences is, surely, the restriction of domesticity, or rather, the projection in the city at large of the functions that in a farmstead would be carried on within the bosom of the family.

When a lad is twenty-four and a lass is eighteen, they are permitted to marry, with the benefit of Christian rites and services, and a decorous avoidance of drunkenness and gluttony after the ceremony. Marriage is a simple matter. There are no dowries to consider, no professional anxieties to face, no housing shortage to keep one from finding a home, and above all, perhaps, no landlord to propitiate with money, since all houses are owned by the city and are granted and assigned to individuals for their use. Virtue and beauty are the only qualities that govern a marriage in Christianopolis. Furniture is provided with the house out of the public store. If in Utopia the families are grouped together in a patriarchal household, such as More himself maintained at Chelsea, in Christianopolis they consist of isolated couples, four, at most six people in all, a woman, a man, and such children as are not yet of school age.

Let us visit a young couple in Christianopolis. We reach the house by way of a street, twenty feet broad, faced by houses with a wide frontage on the street, some forty feet in length, and of from fifteen to twenty-five feet in depth. In our crowded towns, today, where people pay for land by the front foot, the frontage is narrow and the houses are deep; and as a result there is a dreadful insufficiency of light and air; but in Christianopolis, as in some of the older European towns, the houses are built to get a maximum of air and sunlight. If it is raining when we make our visit, a covered walk, five feet wide, supported by columns twelve feet high, will shelter us from the rain.

Our friends live, we shall say, in one of the average apartments; so they have three rooms, a bathroom, a sleeping apartment, and a kitchen. "The middle part within the tower has a little open space with a wide window, where wood and the heavier things are raised aloft by pulleys"—in short, a dumbwaiter. Looking out from the window in the rear, we face a well-kept garden; and if our host is inclined to give us wine, he may let us take our pick from among the cobwebs of a small private cellar in the basement, where such things are kept. If it is a cold day, the furnace is going; or

[89]

if we happen to make our visit in the summer time, the awnings are drawn.

Our host makes apologies, perhaps, for a litter of wood and shavings that occupies a corner of the kitchen, for he has just been putting up a few shelves in his spare time, and has borrowed a kit of tools from the public supply house. (Since he is not a carpenter, he has no need for these tools the rest of the year; and other people can have their turn at them.) Coming from Utopia, one of the things that strikes us is the absence of domestic attendance; and when we ask our hostess about it, she tells us that she will not have anyone to wait upon her until she is confined.

"But isn't there a lot of work for you to do all by yourself?" we shall ask.

"Not for anybody with a college training," she will answer. "You see that our furnishings are quite simple; and since there are no gimcracks to be dusted, no polished tables to be oiled, no carpets to be swept, and nothing in our apartment that is just for show to prove that we can afford to live better than our neighbors, the work is scarcely more than enough to keep one in good health and temper. Of course, cooking meals is always something of a nuisance; and washing up is worse. But my husband and I share the work together, in everything but sewing and washing clothes, and you would be surprised how quickly everything gets done. Work is usually galling when somebody else is taking his ease while one is doing it; but where husband and wife share alike, as in Christianopolis, there is really nothing to it. If you'll stay to dinner, you'll find out how easily it goes. Since you haven't brought your

[90]

rations, my husband will get some cooked meats in the public kitchen, and that will do for all of us."

"No one need be surprised at the rather cramped quarters," Andreæ hastens to interject. "People who house vanity . . . can never live spaciously enough. They burden others and are burdened themselves, and no one measures their necessities, nay even their comforts, easily otherwise than by an unbearable and unmovable mass. Oh, only those persons are rich who have all of which they have real need, who admit nothing else, merely because it is possible to have it in abundance."

Carried to its extreme, you will find this philosophy put once for all in Thoreau's Walden. We have got our bearings in Utopia, I believe, when we have determined what a life abundant consists of, and what will suffice for it.

7

Suppose that our friends have children. During the early years of their life they are in the care of their mother. When they have completed their sixth year, the children are given over to the care of the community, and both sexes continue in school through the stages of childhood, youth, and early maturity. "No parent gives closer or more careful attention to his children than is given here, for the most upright preceptors, men as well as women, are placed over them. Moreover," the parents "can visit their children, even unseen by them, as often as they have leisure. As this is an institution for the public good, it is managed agreeably as a common charge for all the citizens. They see to it that the food is appetizing and whole-

[91]

some, that the couches and beds are clean and comfortable, and that the clothes and attire of the whole body are clean. . . . If diseases of the skin or body are contracted, the individuals are cared for in good time; and to avoid the spreading of infection, they are quarantined."

There is scarcely need to examine the program of study except in its broad outlines. It is enough to observe that "the young men have their study period in the morning, the girls in the afternoon, and matrons as well as learned men are their instructors. . . . The rest of their time is devoted to manual training and domestic art and science, as each one's occupation is assigned to his natural inclination. When they have vacant time they are permitted to engage in honorable physical exercises either in the open spaces of the town or in the field."

Two points, however, deserve our attention. The first is that the school is run as a miniature republic. The second is the calibre of the instructors. "The instructors," says our zealous humanist, "are not men from the dregs of human society nor such as are useless for other occupations, but the choice of all the citizens, persons whose standing in the Republic is known and who very often have access to the highest positions of the state."

The last phrase again transports me back to the modern world. I see this fine humanist ideal budding in another place. This time it is a summer school in the hills of New Hampshire, where the children govern themselves in the classroom, where there is no punishment except temporary exclusion from the group, and where, above all, each instructor is chosen because of his creative practice in the subject which he teaches: a highly gifted composer teaches music, an athlete teaches gymnastics, a poet teaches literature. Then I think of all the casual and wasted talents of people who for little more than the asking would share their love of the arts and sciences with little children, if only those who are in charge of little children were not too blind or too fearful to make use of them. Faraday's classic lectures on the physics of the candle, and Ruskin's addresses to a young ladies' boarding school on the function of literature—such things might be multiplied. It is not the creation of this utopian method that is difficult; for the thing has already been done: what we need is its extension. Then children might come to school as gaily as they do in Peterborough, N. H., on the lush summer mornings; and people would not turn their backs on learning any more than they would turn their backs on life. If anyone thinks that Johann Andreæ's prescription for a teaching staff is an impossible one, let him visit the Peterborough School, and examine its records and achievements.

It remains to record the further stages of learning. The halls of the central citadel are divided into twelve departments, and except for the armory, the archives, the printing establishment, and the treasury, these halls are devoted entirely to the arts and sciences.

There is, to begin with, a laboratory of physical science. "Here the properties of metals, minerals, and vegetables, and even the life of animals, are examined, purified, increased, and united for the use of the human race and in the interests of health. . . . Here men learn to regulate fire, make use of air, value the water, and test the earth."

Next to this laboratory is a Drug Supply House, where a pharmacy is scientifically developed, for the curing of physical disease, and adjoining this is a school of medicine, or as Andreæ reports, "a place given over to anatomy. . . . The value of ascertaining the location of the organs and of assisting the struggles of nature no one would deny, unless he be as ignorant of himself as are the barbarians. . . . The inhabitants of Christianopolis teach their youth the operations of life and the various organs, from the parts of the physical body."

We come now then to a Natural Science laboratory which is in effect a Museum of Natural History, an institution founded in Utopia a century and a half before a partial and inadequate substitute—a mere extension of the curio chamber of a Country House—was presented to an admiring world as the British Museum. "This," as Andreæ says, "cannot be too elegantly described," and I heartily agree with him; for he paints the picture of a museum which the American Museum at New York or South Kensington in London has only begun to realize within the last decade or two of their existence.

"Natural history is here seen painted on the walls in detail, and with greatest skill. The phenomena of the sky, views of the earth in different regions, the different races of men, representations of animals, the forms of growing things, classes of stones and gems, are not only on hand and named, but they even teach and make known their nature and qualities. . . . Truly is not recognition of things of the earth much easier of competent demonstration if illustrative materials are at hand and if there is some guide to the memory? For instruction enters altogether more easily through the eyes than through the ears, and much more pleasantly in the presence of refinement than among the base. They are deceived who think it is impossible to teach except in dark caves and with a gloomy brow. A liberal minded man is never so keen as when he has his instructors on confidential terms."

Going farther, we find a mathematics laboratory and a department of mathematical instruments. The first is "remarkable for its diagrams of the heavens, as the hall of physics for its diagrams of the earth. . . . A chart of the star-studded heavens and a reproduction of the whole shining host above were shown," . . . and also "different illustrations representing tools and machines, small models, figures of geometry; instruments of the mechanical arts, drawn, named, and explained." I cannot help expressing my admiration here for the concrete imagination of this remarkable scholar: he deliberately anticipated, not in the vague, allegorical form that Bacon does, but as lucidly as an architect or a museum curator, the sort of institute which South Kensington, with its Departments of Physical and Natural Science, or perhaps the Smithsonian in America, has just begun to resemble. If our museums had begun with the ideal Andreæ had in mind, instead of with the miscellaneous rubbish which was the nucleus of their collections—and still remains the nucleus in many of the less advanced institutions—the presentation of the sciences would be a more adequate thing than it is.

Does Andreæ leave the fine arts out of his picture? By no means. "Opposite the pharmacy is a very roomy shop for pictorial art, an art in which the city takes the greatest delight. For the city, besides being decorated all over with pictures representing the various phases of the earth, makes use of them especially in the instruction of youth and for rendering learning more easy. . . . Besides, pictures and statues of famous men are to be seen everywhere, an incentive of no mean value to the young for striving to imitate their virtue. . . . At the same time also, the beauty of forms is so pleasing to them that they embrace with a whole heart the inner beauty of virtue itself."

At the summit of art and science we naturally find in Christianopolis the temple of religion. Alas! the hand of Calvin has been busy in Christianopolis—recollect that Andreæ once lived in Geneva and admired its ordinances—and attendance at prayers is compulsory. In order to get an idea of this great circular temple, three hundred sixteen feet in circumference and seventy feet high, we must think of a colossal moving picture theater in a modern metropolis. The comparison is not essentially sacrilegious; and I believe that those who will take the trouble to look below the surface will find without difficulty the common denominator between the profane and the ecclesiastical institution. (Attendance at motion pictures, I must quickly add for the benefit of the future historian, has not yet been made compulsory in the modern metropolis.)

One-half of the temple is where the public gatherings take place; and the other is reserved for the distribution of the sacraments and for music. "At the same time, the sacred comedies, by which they set so much store, and are entertained every three months, are shown in the temple."

We have discussed folk, work, and place in Christianopolis; and we have dealt in an admittedly sketchy fashion with culture and art. We must now turn attention to the polity; and here we must note that Andreæ's description shifts for once to an allegorical plane, and departs not a little from the realism of his treatment of science and the arts.

At the bottom of the polity there are glimpses of a local industrial association, meeting in the common halls that are provided in the towers of each of the industrial quarters; and we gather that to represent the city at large twenty-four councilmen are chosen, while as the executive department there is a triumvirate consisting of a Minister, a Judge, and a Director of Learning, each of whom is married, for metaphorical point, to Conscience, Understanding, and Truth, respectively. "Each one of the leaders does his own duty, yet not without the knowledge of others; all consult together in matters that concern the safety of the state."

In the censorship of books, Christianopolis reminds us of the Republic; in the exclusion of lawyers it calls up nearly every other utopia; and in its attitude towards crime it has a temperance and leniency that is all its own, for "the judges of this Christian city observe this custom especially, that they punish most severely those misdeeds which are directed straight against God, less severely those which injure men, and lightest of all those who harm only property. As the Christian citizens are always chary of spilling blood,

[97]

they do not willingly agree upon the death sentence as a form of punishment. . . . For anyone can destroy a man but only the best can reform."

How shall we sum up this government? Let Andreæ speak his own words; for he has reached the innermost shrine of Christianopolis and perceives the center of activity in the state.

"Here religion, justice, and learning have their abode, and theirs is the control of the city. . . I often wonder what people mean who separate and disjoint their best powers, the joining of which might render them blessed as far as may be on earth. There are those who would be considered religious, who throw off all things human; there are some who are pleased to rule, though without any religion at all; learning makes a great noise, flattering now this one, now that, yet applauding itself most. What finally may the tongue do except provoke God, confuse men, and destroy itself? So there would seem to be a need of co-operation which only Christianity can give—Christianity which conciliates God with men and unites men together, so that they have pious thoughts, do good deeds, know the truth, and finally die happily to live eternally."

There are some who might object to this statement on the ground that it smacked too heartily of supernatural religion; but it remains just as valid if we translate it into terms whose theological reactions have been neutralized. To have a sense of values, to know the world in which they are set, and to be able to distribute them—this is our modern version of Andreæ's conception of religion, learning, and justice. A little search might uncover another expression of the Human ist ideal as complete and magnificent as this; but I doubt if it would find a better one. In essence, this blunt and forthright German scholar is standing shoulder to shoulder with Plato: his Christianopolis is as enduring as the best nature of men.

CHAPTER FIVE

How Bacon and Campanella, who have a great reputation as utopians, are little better than echoes of the men who went before them.

CHAPTER FIVE

1

A GENOESE sea-captain is the guest of a Grand Master of the Knights Hospitaller. This sea-captain tells him of a great country under the equator, dominated by the City of the Sun. The outward appearance of this country is a little strange—the city with its seven rings named after the seven planets, and its four gates that lead to the four quarters of the earth, and the hill that is topt by a grand temple, and the walls covered with laws and alphabets and paintings of natural phenomena, and the Rulers—Power, Wisdom, and Love—with the learned doctors, Astrologus, Cosmographus, Arithmeticus, and their like: it is an apparition such as never yet was seen on land or sea. Small wonder, for this City of the Sun existed only in the exotic brain of a Calabrian monk, Tommaso Campanella, whose Utopia existed in manuscript before Andreæ wrote his Christianopolis.

We shall not stay long in the City of the Sun. After we have become familiar with the outward color and form of the landscape, we discover, alas! that it is not a foreign country we are exploring, but a sort of picture puzzle put together out of fragments from Plato and More. As in the Republic, there is a complete community of property, a community of wives, and an equality of the sexes; as in Utopia, the younger people wait upon the elders; as in Christianopolis, science is imparted, or at least hinted at, by demonstration. When one subtracts what these other Utopian countries have contributed, very little indeed remains.

But we must not neglect to observe two significant passages. One of them is the recognition of the part that invention might play in the ideal commonwealth. The people of the City of the Sun have wagons that are driven by the wind, and boats "which go over the waters without rowers or the force of the wind, but by a marvelous contrivance." There is a very clear anticipation of the mechanical improvements which began to multiply so rapidly in the eighteenth century. At the tale end of the sea-captain's recital, the Grand Master exclaims: "Oh, if you knew what our astrologers say of the coming age, that has in it more history within a hundred years than all the world had in four thousand years before! Of the wonderful invention of printing and guns, and the use of the magnet. . . . " With the mechanical arts in full development, labor in the City of the Sun has become dignified: it is not the custom to keep slaves. Since everyone takes his part in the common work, there is not more than four hours' work to be done per day. "They are rich because they want nothing; poor because they possess nothing; and consequently they are not slaves to circumstances, but circumstances serve them."

The other point upon which Campanella's observation is remarkably keen is his explanation of the relation of private property and the private household to the commonwealth. Thus:

"They say that all private property is acquired and improved for the reason that each one of us by himself has his own home and wife and children. From this self-love springs. For when we raise a son to riches and dignities, and leave an heir to much wealth, we become either ready to grasp at the property of the state, if in any case fear should be removed from the power which belongs to riches and rank; or avaricious, crafty, and hypocritical, if any is of slender purse, little strength, and mean ancestry. But when we have taken away self-love, there remains only love for the state."

How shall the common Utopia keep from being neglected through each one's concern for his little private utopia?

This is the critical problem that our utopians have all to face; and Campanella loyally follows Plato in his solution. It is perhaps inevitable that each utopian's personal experience of life should enter into his solution, and overwhelmingly give it color; and here the limitations of our utopians are plain. More and Andreæ are married men, and they stand for the individual family. Plato and Campanella were bachelors, and they proposed that men should live like monks or soldiers. Perhaps these two camps are not so far away as they would seem. If we follow the exposition of that excellent anthropologist, Professor Edward Westermarck, we shall be fairly well convinced, I believe, that marriage is a biological institution, and thorough promiscuity is, to say the least, an unusual form of mating. Plato perhaps recognized this when he left us in doubt as to whether a community of wives would be practiced by his artisans and husbandmen. So he perhaps paves the way for a solution by which the normal life for the great majority of men would be marriage, with its individual concerns and loyalties, whilst for the active,

[105]

creative elements in the community a less secluded form of mating would be practiced. The painter, Van Gogh, has given us a kernel to chew on when he says that the sexual life of the artist must be either that of the monk or the soldier, for otherwise he is distracted from his creative work.

We may leave this question in the air, as long as we realize that all our utopias rest upon our ability to discover some sort of a solution.

2

Francis Bacon's New Atlantis is not a utopia in the sense that I have explained our principle of selection in the preface to the bibliography. It is only a fragment, and not very good as fragments go; and it would drop out altogether from our survey were it not for the hugely over-rated reputation that Bacon has as a philosopher of natural science—indeed, as *the* philosopher after Aristotle.

The greater part of Bacon's ideas are anticipated and more amply expressed by Andreæ. When we have deleted Bacon's multitudinous prayers and exhortations, when we have disposed of his copious descriptions of jewels and velvets and satins and ceremonial regalia, we find that the core of his commonwealth is Salomon's House, sometimes known as the College of the Six Days' Works; which he describes as the noblest foundation that ever was upon earth, and the lantern of the kingdom.

The purpose of this foundation is the "knowledge of the causes and secret motions of things; and the enlarging of the bounds of human empire, to the effecting of all things possible." The material resources of this foundation are manifold. It has laboratories dug into the sides of hills, and observatories with towers half a mile high; it has great lakes of salt and fresh water which seem to anticipate the marine laboratories we know today; and it has engines for setting things in motion. Besides this, there are spacious houses where physical demonstrations are made, and sanatoria where various novel cures are attempted; there are experimental agricultural stations, too, where grafts and crosses are tried. Add to this pharmaceutical laboratories, industrial laboratories, and numerous houses devoted to such things as experiments with sounds, lights, perfumes, and tastes—which Bacon presents in a wild farrago without any regard to the essential sciences to which the work he describes is related—and one has a tally of the "riches of Salomon's House."

Twelve fellows of the college travel into foreign lands to bring back books and abstracts, and reports on experiments and inventions. Three make a digest of experiments. Three collect the experiments of all the mechanical arts, and also of practices which are not brought into the arts. Three try new experiments. Three devote themselves to classifications; and another three, known as dowry men or benefactors, look into the experiments of their fellows and cast about for means of applying them to human life and knowledge. Three fellows consult with the whole body of scientific workers and plan new channels of investigation; and three, who are called interpreters of nature, attempt to raise the results of particular investigations into general observations and axioms.

In telling all this, as in the rest of his New Atlantis,

Bacon is incredibly childish and incoherent: he gives such a description of Salomon's House as a six-year-old schoolboy might give of a visit to the Rockefeller Foundation. Beneath these maladroit interpretations, however, we see that Bacon had a grasp on some of the fundamentals of scientific research, and of the part that science might play in the "relief of man's estate." It is nothing more than a hint, this New Atlantis; but a word to the wise is enough; and as we look about the modern world we see that, in its material affairs at any rate, the great scientific institutes and foundations—the United States Bureau of Standards, for one—play a part not a little like that of the College of the Six Days' Works.

Campanella with his dream of powerful mechanical inventions, in which he had been anticipated by Leonardo, and Bacon with his sketch of scientific institutes—with these two utopians we stand at the entrance to the utopia of means; that is to say, the place in which all that materially contributes to the good life has been perfected. The earlier utopias were concerned to establish the things which men should aim for in life. The utopias of the later Renascence took these aims for granted and discussed how man's scope of action might be broadened. In this the utopians only reflected the temper of their time; and did not attempt to remold it. As a result of our preoccupation with the means, we in the Western World live in an inventor's paradise. Scientific knowledge and mechanical power we have to burn; more knowledge and more power than Bacon or Campanella could possibly have dreamed of. But today we face again the riddle that Plato, More, and

Andreæ sought to answer: what are men to do with their knowledge and power?

As we skip here and there through the Utopias of the next three centuries, this question gets more deeply impregnated in our minds.

CHAPTER SIX

How something happened in the eighteenth century which made men "furiously to think," and how a whole group of utopias sprang out of the upturned soil of industrialism.

CHAPTER SIX

1

THERE is a gap in the Utopian tradition between the seventeenth century and the nineteenth. Utopia, the place that must be built, faded into no-man's land, the spot to which one might escape; and the utopias of Denis Vayrasse and Simon Berington and the other romancers of this in-between period are in the line of Robinson Crusoe rather than the Republic.

One finds the clue to this lapse in Tiphaigne de la Roche's Giphantia, a sketch of what was and what is and what will be, and in particular, an inquiry into the "Babylonian" mode of life. The author of Giphantia tells a parable about Sophia, the incarnation of Wisdom, who rejects the offers of the spendthrift, the merchant, the soldier, and the student, and accepts the suit of a diffident fellow who had retired in solitude to the country, to spend his days like a cultivated gentleman. One remembers the way in which Montaigne spent his declining years; one remembers Voltaire; and one sees how deeply the ideal of Robinson Crusoe—a cultivated Robinson Crusoe, surrounded with books and beyond the reach of any king and court—colored the deepest aspirations of this period. Rousseau, writing about the corrupting influence of the arts and sciences, and Chateaubriand, seeking the noble savage in the American wilderness and finding him in his own bosom—these men struck the dominating note of the eighteenth century. In a society that was already painfully artificial and "arranged" the institutes of Lycurgus and Utopus must have seemed as repressive as those of Louis XIV. So almost two centuries pass before we find any fresh regions to explore in Utopia.

2

The Utopia of Sir Thomas More, and those of the later men of the Renascence, arose, as I have pointed out, from the contrast between the possibilities that lay open beyond the sea and the dismal conditions that attended the breakdown of the town economy of the Middle Age. Like Plato's Republic, it attempted to face the difficult problem of transition.

In the course of the next three centuries the adventure of exploring and ransacking strange countries loses its hold upon men's imagination; and a new type of activity becomes the center of interest. The conquest of alien countries and the lure of gold do not indeed die out with this new interest; but they are subordinated to another type of conquest—that which man seeks to effect over nature. Here and there, particularly in Great Britain, untrained men "with a practical turn" begin to busy themselves with improving the mechanical appartus by which the day's labor is done. A retired barber, named Arkwright, invents a spinning frame, a Scotchman named MacAdam discovers a new method of laying roads; and out of a hundred such inventions during the late eighteenth and early nineteenth centuries a new world comes into existence—a world in which energy derived from coal and running water takes the place of human

[114]

energy; in which goods manipulated by machinery take the place of goods woven or sawed or hammered by hand. Within a hundred years the actual world and the idola were transformed.

In this new world of falling water, burning coal, and whirring machinery, utopia was born again. It is easy to see why this should have happened, and why about two-thirds of our utopias should have been written in the nineteenth century. The world was being visibly made over; and it was possible to conceive of a different order of things without escaping to the other side of the earth. There were political changes, and the monarchic state was tempered by republicanism; there were industrial changes, and two hungry mouths were born where one could feed before; and there were social changes—the strata of society shifted and "faulted," and men who in an earlier period would have been doomed to a dull and ignominious round, perhaps, took a place alongside those whom inheritance had given all the privileges of riches and breeding.

In contrast to all these fresh possibilities were the dismal realities which were easily enough perceived by people who stood outside this new order, or who by temperament revolted against the indignities and repressions and vilenesses that accompanied it. It is not my particular business here to deal with the facts of history; but unless one understands the facts of history, the utopias which I am about to present lose a good part of their meaning. Those machines whose output was so great that all men might be clothed; those new methods of agriculture and new agricultural implements, which promised crops so big that all men might be fed—the very instruments that were to give the whole community the physical basis of a good life turned out, for the vast majority of people who possessed neither capital nor land, to be nothing short of instruments of torture.

I do not speak too harshly of the early industrial age; it is impossible to speak too harshly. Take the trouble to read Robert Owen's "Essay on the Formation of Character" (Manchester: 1837) and learn what conditions were like in a model factory run by an enlightened employer: it is a picture of unmitigated brutality. One must go back to the blackest periods of ancient slavery for a parallel, if indeed one would find it, for the Pyramids that were built under the lash have a certain grandeur and permanence which justify their existence, whilst the goods which were produced in Yorkshire through the maimed bodies of pauper children proved to be as impermanent as the lives that were sacrificed in making them.

Those who were inside this new order—the Gradgrinds and Bounderbys whom Dickens pictures in "Hard Times"—sought to realize their utopia of the Iron Age on earth. When we are through with the genuine utopians we shall examine the idola by which all the "practical" men of the nineteenth century, Marx as well as Macaulay, patterned their behavior. Those who stood out against this new order were not so much opposed to the new methods as to the purposes for which they were being used: they felt that an orderly conquest of Nature had turned into a wild scramble for loot, and that all the goods industrialism promised were being lost, for the benefit of a few aggressive and unsocialized individuals. With the host of critics and interpreters and reformers that arose in the nineteenth

[116]

century we shall have a little reckoning to make presently: those who concern us here however belong to the stock of Plato, More, and Andreæ, in that they attempted to see society as a whole, and to protect a new order which would be basically sound as well as superficially improved. Yet with the exception of the utopias which revolted against industrialism these nineteenth century essays are partial and one-sided; for they tend to magnify the importance of the industrial order as much as Gradgrind and Bounderby did, and in doing this they lose sight of the whole life of man. These industrial utopias are no longer concerned with values but with means; they are all instrumentalist. I doubt whether an intelligent peasant in India or China would get out of the whole batch of these utopias a single idea which would have any bearing on the life that he has experienced—so little of human significance remains when the problems of mechanical and political organization have been disposed of!

One symptom of this lack of individuality, this lack of what, in the old-fashioned sense used to be called a philosophy, is the fact that we can treat all these industrial utopias in groups. The first of these group-utopias I shall call, perhaps somewhat arbitrarily, the Associationists.

3

Among the Associationists, the most influential utopian is Charles François Marie Fourier. He was a prolific and incoherent writer, and his Utopia, if the truth be told, exists as disjecta membra rather than as a single work; but in his case I make an exception to the criterion of selection; because in every other respect he has a claim upon our attention. This Fourier was a dry little French commercial traveller, whose personal fortune was lost in the French revolution and whose hopes for founding a real eutopia were blasted by the July revolution of 1830. Again and again he transferred himself from one line of goods to another in order to increase the area of the territory he covered and learn more of the workings of society; and so in his writings a wealth of concrete detail goes hand in hand with personal crotchets and the opinionativeness which arises almost inevitably out of an undisciplined solitude. What follows is a distillation of Fourier's thought, with the lees and orts left in the bottom of the flask.

Fourier differs largely from the early utopians in that he is concerned first of all not with modifying human nature but with finding out what it actually is. His utopia is to be based upon an understanding of man's actual physical and mental makeup, and its institutions are to be such as will permit man's original nature to function freely. The motive which draws his community together is attraction; the power which sets his institutions going is "the passions." Under the head of passions—the original biological equipment—Fourier gives a list of tendencies which corresponds roughly with the modern psychologist's list of instincts.

Fourier takes these passions as "given"; his utopia is not designed to "effect any change in our passions . . . their direction will be changed without changing their nature." As Brisbane says in his Introduction to Fourier's philosophy, social institutions are to these passional forces what machinery is to material forces. A good community, according to

[118]

Fourier, is one which will bring all these passions into play, in their complex actions and interactions.

As in the Republic, the ideal behind Fourier's utopia is harmony; for man has a threefold destiny; namely, "an industrial destiny, to harmonize the material world; a social destiny, to harmonize the passional or moral world; and an intellectual destiny, to discover the laws of universal order and harmony." What was at fault with modern civilized societies was that they were incomplete, and in their functioning they created a social dissonance. To overcome this, says Fourier, men must unite into harmonious associations which will give play to all their activities, and which, by erecting common institutions, will do away with the waste arising in the individual's attempts to do for himself all the things which would be done by a complete community.

For this perfect association Fourier provides minute plans and tables; but the general plan can be outlined with brevity.

First of all, Fourier, too, goes back to the valley section. The initial nucleus of his utopia is to consist of a company of 1,500 or 1,600 persons, owning a good stretch of land comprising at least a square league. Since this experimental phalanx, as Fourier called it, would have to stand alone, and without the support of neighboring phalanxes, there will in consequence of this isolation be many gaps in "attraction," and "many passional calms to dread in its workings." To overcome this, Fourier insists that it is necessary to locate the phalanx on soil fit for a variety of functions. "A flat country, such as Antwerp, Leipsic, Orleans, would be totally unsuitable . . . owing to the uniformity of land surface. It will therefore be necessary to select

[119]

a diversified region, like the surroundings of Lausanne, or at the very least, a fine valley, provided with a stream of water and a forest, like the valley of Brussel or of Halle."

This domain would be laid out in fields, orchards, vineyards, and so forth, according to the nature' of the soil and industrial requirements. By devotion to horticulture and arboriculture, Fourier figures, an intensive development would supply abundantly the needs of the colony. The main economic occupation of the phalanx would be agricultural—this is perhaps the great distinction between Fourier and later Utopians—but all the arts would be practiced within the phalanstery, since otherwise the association would be incomplete.

The principle of the association is concretely embodied in a vast edifice in the center of the domain: "a palace complete in all its appointments serving as the residence of the associates. In this palace there are three wings, corresponding to the Material, the Social, and the Intellectual domains. In one wing are the workshops and halls of industry. In another are the library, the scientific collections, museums, artists' studios, and the like. In the center, devoted to the social element, are banquet halls, a hall of reception, and grand salons. At one end of the palace is a Temple of the Material Harmonies, devoted to singing, music, poetry, dancing, gymnastics, painting, and so forth. At the other end is the Temple of Unityism, to celebrate with appropriate rites man's unity with the universe. On the summit there is an observatory with telegraph and signal tower, for communication with other phalanxes.

The phalanx men are associationists; but it follows

[120]

from Fourier's theory of the passions that they have private interests as well as public ones; and these private interests are permitted to flourish as long as they do not interfere with social solidarity. Thus they avoid the waste inherent in private housekeeping by having public kitchens, where, incidentally, the children are trained from an early age at cooking, as they are today in one or two experimental schools: nevertheless it is possible to dine in solitude as well as in company. By the same token, every member of the phalanx is guaranteed a minimum of food, clothing, lodging, and even amusements without respect to work; at the same time, private property is sanctioned, and each member extracts from the common store a dividend in proportion to the amount of stock he holds in the association. This dividend, it must be qualified, is considerably reduced by the fact that a system of profit sharing replaces the pure wage system. There is thus a sort of balance between private self-seeking and the maintenance of the public good.

In order to manufacture goods economically, large scale production is introduced wherever possible, and the division of labor is forced to its ultimate limits. Fourier takes account of the resulting monotony, however, and suggests that the monotony be corrected by having recourse to changing tasks and occupations from time to time. In commercial exchange, the phalanx acts as a unit; it constitutes a great self-governing body which traffics in surplus goods with similar associations, without any middleman, in something of the manner, perhaps, that the Co-operative Wholesale Societies do today.

By abolishing the individual household, the phalanx

gives a new freedom to women; and Fourier does not
see how it is possible to maintain the system of mono-
gamic proprietorship once women have a free choice
of mates. So the women of the phalanx are not intellectual nonentities; and since they no longer preside over the individual home, they help run the whole
community. Is it necessary to add the common
nurseries, the common schools, the informal education
of the children, and the number of other things which
follow from this emancipation?

Perhaps one of the most remarkable characteristics
of this utopia is its utilization of a moral equivalent
for war, long before Professor William James invented
the phrase. One of the great functions of the phalanx
is the assemblage of productive armies even as "civilization" assembles destructive ones. There is a fine
passage in which Fourier pictures an industrial army
of golden youths and maidens, "instead of devastating
thirty provinces in a campaign, these armies will have
spanned thirty rivers with bridges, re-wooded thirty
barren mountains, dug thirty trenches for irrigation,
and drained thirty marshes." It is for lack of such
industrial armies, says Fourier, that civilization is unable to produce anything great.

4

What strikes us when we put together the fragments
of Fourier's utopia—as one might put together a jig-
saw puzzle—is the fact that he faces the variety and
inequality of human nature. Instead of erecting a
standard for men to live up to, and rejecting mankind
as unfit for utopia because the standard is far beyond

[122]

its height, the standard itself is founded upon the utmost capacity which a community might be able to exhibit. Fourier meets human nature half-way: he endeavors to project a society which will give regular channels to all its divergent impulses, and prevent them from spilling unsocially all over the landscape. In his statement of this aim there are plenty of weaknesses and absurdities; and I confess that it is hard to take this pathetic little man seriously; but when one has grappled with Fourier's thought one discovers that there is something to take.

Fourier died without persuading anyone to give a trial to his scheme of association; and yet his work was not without its practical influence. The Brook Farm experiment in America was a fumbling attempt to plant a phalanstery without paying any attention to the conditions which Fourier would have rigorously imposed; and the "familistere" of the great steel works of Godin at Guise, in France, is another direct result of Fourier's inspiration. He remains, I believe, the first man who had a plan for colonizing the wilderness of industrial barbarism that existed at the beginning of the nineteenth century, and redeeming that wilderness to civilization.

5

The name of Robert Owen is usually associated with utopianism; but his work belongs more to the "real" world than to the idola of utopia; and I pass over him with the briefest mention, for his projects for a model industrial town have more of the flavor of a poor colony than that of a productive human society. Let us grant him good intentions, organizing ability, and moral fervor: without doubt he is a noble figure, even when his attitude is strained and his tone strident. The series of essays he wrote on love and marriage are marked by fine sympathy and common sense; and it is to be regretted that they are not as widely known as his plans for a new moral world. If this little note can repair the neglect, I have done Owen ample justice: as an active figure in English and American public life he is properly a subject for the social historian. With Owen I must also dismiss John Ruskin, who began in the last quarter of the nineteenth century to develop plans for a "Guild of St. George." This guild was to form a little island of honest labor and sound education in the midst of the turbid sea of industrialism; but it did not embrace the whole of society, and it was utopian only in the sense that the Oneida Community, let us say, was utopian. While they are full of pregnant suggestions, the plans for the Guild are as fragmentary as the New Atlantis.

6

One of the neglected utopias of the mid-nineteenth century is that of James Buckingham.

James Buckingham was one of those erratic men of affairs which the fertile soil of British individualism produces, and which hard British common sense persistently ignores. Like Owen, Buckingham was acquainted with industrial and commercial affairs from the inside: he travelled widely and wrote upon various matters with that copious, amateurish dogmatism and spirit which marks him, perhaps, as the philistine counterpart of John Ruskin. If the utopias of the past express the ideals of the soldier, the farmer, and

[124]

the artisan, the community which Buckingham projected represents the ideal of the bourgeoisie. Buckingham's Victoria is the ideal aspect of that Coketown which in a later chapter we shall attempt to describe.

We talk loosely of the individualism of the nineteenth century; but in reality it was a period that was thriving with associations. The scope of joint stock companies and philanthropic societies had immeasurably widened. Along with the Mudfog Association, "for the advancement of everything," which Dickens satirized, there sprang up a hundred different societies for performing some special function in the industrial system or realizing some particular purpose in society. Buckingham gives us a picture of his contemporaries which is also a criticism:

"We have the government of the country itself, passing acts of parliament for the better drainage of towns, and a more ample supply of water and air for ventilation. . . . Hence, too, arise associations of noblemen and others for building model lodging houses for the labouring classes; associations for improving the dwellings of the poor; societies for providing baths and bath houses for families unable to procure such conveniences for themselves; associations for establishing suburban villages for the working classes, and to get them at night at least out of the crowded haunts and vicious atmosphere of the towns. And hence we have Temperance Societies, Tract Societies, Home Missions, Asylums for Repentant Magdalens, Homes for Seaman out of Employ, and Houses of Refuge for the Destitute, with soup kitchens and other modes of temporary relief. . . ."

[125]

What does this all come to? Let Buckingham answer:

"They are, after all, mere palliatives, and do not reach the seat of the disease. . . . This can only be done by uniting the disjointed efforts of all these well-meaning but partially curative bodies into one, in order to achieve, by their union of means, influence, and example, the erection of a "Model Society," with its model farms, model pastures, model mines, model manufactures, model town, model schools, model workshops, model kitchens, model libraries, and places of recreation, enjoyment, and instruction; all of which could be united in one new Association."

Without inquiring too closely into what a model pasture may be, we may admit that the notion behind Buckingham's proposal was not unsound. The industrial society of his day was in an inchoate, indeed in a chaotic state. In order to sift out the necessary institutions and put them on a firm basis, it was the better part of wisdom to start anew on a fresh area of land and attempt to plan the development of the community as a whole. It is true that in this proposal of Buckingham's there is none of Fourier's brilliant intuitions of a true social order, and none of Ruskin's critical inquiry into what composed a good life: Buckingham took contemporary values for granted. What he sought to do was to realize these values completely, and in orderly fashion. Here are the elements of his proposal.

There is to be formed a model town association, with a limited liability, for the purpose of building a new town called Victoria. The town is to contain every improvement in "position, plan, drainage, ventilation, architecture, supply of water, light, and every other elegance and convenience." Its size is to be about a mile square and the number of inhabitants is not to exceed 10,000. A suitable variety of manufactures and handicraft trades is to be established near the edge of the town; and the town itself is to be surrounded by farm land 10,000 acres broad. All of the lands, houses, factories, and materials are to be the property of the company, and not of any individual; and this property is to be held for the benefit of all in proportion as their shares entitle them. No person is to be a member of the company or an inhabitant of the town except one who is a bona fide shareholder to the extent of at least twenty pounds, and who is ready to subscribe to a drastic series of blue laws which, while permitting freedom in religious worship and preventing child labor, do away with liquor, drugs, and even tobacco.

In addition to these provisions there are to be common laundries, kitchens, refectories, and nurseries; and medical advice is to be given free, at home or in the hospital, as in the army and navy. Education is to be undertaken by the community. Justice, it should be noted by those who are acquainted with an experiment which has recently been started in New York, is to be administered by competent arbitrators under a written code of laws, without the expense, delay, and uncertainty of ordinary legal proceedings. All members are to sign declarations accepting arbitration and waiving other legal proceedings against members of the company.

All these affairs, especially the manner in which the town is to be built, are worked out in considerable detail; thus the size and character of the houses are set

forth on the plan, and it is provided that each working-
man is to occupy at least one entire and separate
room for himself; whilst each married couple without
children gets two rooms, and each family in which there
are children is to occupy at least three rooms for domestic purposes. I have set down all these details
baldly because the plan itself is a bald one; and no
amount of fine writing will embellish it. Buckingham's
society is not based upon a thoroughgoing criticism of
human institutions: the ends for which this society
exists are doubtless those which were held good and
proper by the Macaulays and the Martineaus. What
is interesting in Buckingham's utopia is the definite
plans and specifications, accompanied by drawings; for
this is surely one of the first attempts to put a problem in social engineering on a basis from which an
engineer or an architect could work.

Buckingham thought that, given a successful model
town, the rest of England might in time be colonized
by the surplus population, and thus the old centers of
black industry would be wiped out. Nor was Buckingham altogether deceived. His utopia was a limited one,
but out of his limitations has come success. In 1848
this utopia was a chimera; in 1898, Mr. Ebenezer
Howard reconstructed it and set it forth in a persuasive
little book called Tomorrow, and as a direct result of
the plans advocated by Mr. Howard, a flourishing
garden city called Letchworth has come into existence;
which in turn has propagated another garden city,
called Wellwyn; and at the same time has, by example,
paved the way for numerous garden villages and
garden suburbs in various parts of Europe and in
America.

With this mid-Victorian theorist, we pass over from a pre-scientific method of thinking to one which sacrifices the artistic imagination to a realistic grasp of the facts; and in this passage something is gained and something is lost. Buckingham gains by confining his proposals to what is immediately practicable. He loses by not having the imaginative energy to criticize the ways, means, and ends that are sanctioned by current practise. If utopia begins with Plato's glorious dream of an organic community, the image of the just man made perfect, it cannot end with Buckingham's invention of a shell. Nevertheless, through the nineteenth century the superficial utopians, the shell-builders, are dominant; and we must continue to examine them.

CHAPTER SEVEN

How some utopians have thought that a good community rested at bottom on the right division and use of land; and what sort of communities these land-animals projected.

CHAPTER SEVEN

1

BEFORE the Industrial Revolution upset the balance of social power, there were little villages in England where, on a limited scale and to no very grand purpose, a quiet and placid and fairly jolly existence must have been the rule of things. These villages were those in which the land was either held in freehold by small proprietors, or where there still remained for the use of each inhabitant certain common pastures and wastes. Under this regime there was a fair degree of prosperity with which only the wind and the weather and war could interfere. Something of the savor of this life Mr. W. H. Hudson finely conveys in his A Traveller in Little Things; and a century ago Cobbett made a series of excellent snapshots in his Rural Rides.

When the mediæval order broke down the great proprietors began to seize this common land; and during the eighteenth century, under the incentive of big-scale scientific agriculture, the seizure went on at a merry pace. The peasant without land was forced to migrate to the new towns, as the Hammonds have pictured in their graphic work on the Town Laborer; and the labor of the peasant and his family fed the machines which the Watts and Arkwrights were developing in the eighteenth century. Industrial progress and social poverty went hand in hand. The period before the

[133]

Industrial Revolution seemed in comparison a real utopia; and the key to this utopia was the land.

The importance of land in the constitution of civil society was emphasized by the Diggers of Cromwell's time; one of them, Gerard Winstanley, wrote a minor utopia to prove that the land should be held in common; and this view was reinforced—without the communism—in a purely political utopia called Oceana by James Harrington, who lived during the same period. Harrington advocated such a distribution of land that the landed gentry should be the leaders, and the commonalty should have the preponderance of power.

Out of all the modern utopias with which we have to reckon there are two, in particular, in which the common possession of land is the foundation of every other institution. These are Spensonia and A Visit to Freeland.

2

The early part of the nineteenth century is remarkable for the fact that men of common stock, usually self-educated, began to apply their wits to improving the conditions of the class to which they belonged; and in particular there was in London a peasant named William Cobbett, a tailor named Francis Place, and a stationer named Thomas Spence who devoted a good part of what remained over from their working days to plans for bettering man's estate.

Thomas Spence had a shop in High Holborn from which he published little pamphlets of rough philosophy, called Pig's Meat; in 1795 he issued A Description of Spensonia, which was followed in 1801 by The

Constitution of Spensonia: A Country in Fairyland situated between Utopia and Oceana; brought from thence by Captain Swallow. Spence's title to have written a complete utopia rests upon the fact that he proposes a return to an environment which had once been, in its fashion, complete.

Spensonia begins with a parable about a father who had a number of sons, who built them a ship for traffic, and who provided that the profits of the enterprise were to be shared in common. This ship is wrecked upon an island; and the sons quickly awake to the conclusion that if "they did not apply the Marine Constitution given them by their father to their landed property, they would soon experience inexpressible inconveniences. They therefore declared the property of the island to be the property of them all collectively, in the same manner as the ship had been, and that they ought to share the profits thereof in the same way. The island they named Spensonia, after the ship which their father had given them. They next chose officers to mark out such portions of the land, as every person or family desired to occupy, for which they were to receive for the use of the public a certain rent according to its value. This rent was applied to public uses or divided among themselves as they thought proper. But in order to keep up the remembrance of their rights, they decreed that they should never fail to share at rent-time, an equal dividend, though ever so small, and though the public demands should be ever so urgent. . . . As they had determined, when seeing that every ship they should build and man, should . . . be the property of the crew, so, in conformity therewith, they decreed that every district or parish which they should people, should be the property of the inhabitants, and the rent and police of the same at their disposal. . . . A National Assembly or Congress consisting of delegates from all the parishes takes care of the national concerns, and defrays the expenses of the state and matters of common utility, by a pound rate from each parish without any other tax."

What is a parish and what is its work? Look around the English countryside and see.

A parish, to begin with, is a "compact portion of the country, designedly not too large that it may the more easily be managed by the inhabitants with respect to its revenues and the police."

"The parishes build and repair houses, make roads, plant hedges and trees, and in a word do all the business of a landlord. . . . A parish has many heads to contrive what ought to be done. Instead of debating about mending the state, . . . (for ours needs no mending) we employ our ingenuity nearer home, and the result of the debates are in every parish, how we shall work such a mine, make such a river navigable, drain such a fen, or improve such a waste. These things we are all immediately interested in, and have each a vote in executing."

There is a rough, homespun quality about this utopia, and it needs a visit to the English villages of the New Forest or the Chiltern Hills, where some of the common lands have been kept, to see what a rural utopia would be like if it could keep itself free from invaders who sought to live off the fat of the land without contributing their labor. Spence was not altogether blind to the necessity of keeping watch over this constitution of equality; and he places his utopia in the care of two guardian angels—Voting by Ballot and the Universal Use of Arms—two angels which look less formidable and potent in the twentieth century than they did in the first decade of the nineteenth, when the first had still to be tried, and when the second was not complicated by the invention of machine guns and poison gases.

At the bottom of Spence's Utopia, however, lies the conviction which he shares with Plato and all the other genuine utopians; namely, that in Thoreau's words less is accomplished by the thousands who are hacking at the branches of evil than by one who is striking at the root. Spence, it must be remembered, wrote in the thick of the agitation for parliamentary reform which was the keynote of so much nineteenth century activity —the chartist movement, parliamentary socialism, and the like, being so many rainbows in the bubble of political effort which burst with such a bang when the Great War broke out. Spence saw the futility of these superficial demands. He said:

"Thousands of abortive schemes are daily proposed for redressing grievances and mending the constitution, whereas, the shoes were so ill-made at first, and so worn, rotten, and patched already, that they are not worth the trouble or expense, but ought to be thrown to the dunghill; and a new pair should be made, neat, tight, and easy as for the foot of one that loves freedom and ease. Then would your controversies about this and the other way of cobbling, that continually agitate you, be done away; and you would walk along the rugged and dirty path of life easy and dry-shod."

[137]

The next utopia, Freeland, marks a transition between the utopia in which the land alone is held by the community and that in which land and capital and all the machinery of production belong to a national state.

The writer of this utopia was an Austrian economist, Theodor Hertzka; and he first published his view in considerable detail, with reference to current economic doctrines, in a book called Freeland: A Social Anticipation. He condensed these doctrines in another book called A Visit to Freeland, or the new Paradise Regained, an attempt to picture his freeman's commonwealth in action.

These books formed the center of a whirlwind of agitation; a magazine sprang up; societies were organized in various cities in Europe and America; and a definite attempt was made to colonize a certain section of Africa, selected by Hertzka; an attempt which, alas! met with speedy failure as a result of the obtuseness and international jealousy of various colonial officials. The first book was published in 1889; and all this happened in the early nineties. Perhaps the only practical effect of it was—and this is mere conjecture—to turn the thoughts of certain Zionists, like Israel Zangwill, from establishing Zion in Jerusalem to building it up again in some more suitable region in the heart of Africa.

Freeland may be described as an individualist Utopia on a social foundation. Hertzka was filled with sympathy and admiration for the doctrines that Adam Smith set forth in The Wealth of Nations; and he de-

sired to realize a society in which the maximum amount
of individual freedom and initiative would prevail, especially in industrial enterprises. This leads to a
paradox; namely, that in order to ensure freedom it
is impossible to practise laissez faire; for the effect of
laissez faire is to permit accidental aggregations of
wealth and power to threaten the freedom that less
fortunate individuals seek to enjoy. So far from
being an anarchist utopia, Freeland is a co-operative
commonwealth in which the State acts as an interested
party in the production and distribution of goods. This
differs from socialism in name; and it differed from the
practical socialist agitation of the time in that it re-
lied, not upon turning over established institutions in
Europe, but in turning over a new leaf in the Kenia
Highlands of Africa; but Hertzka's "individualism"
comes to almost the same thing.

4

A visit to Freeland teaches us little about the arts
of social life or the constitution of a good society.
What we can learn is one of the methods by which—
on hypothesis anyway—the industrial mechanism
might be controlled.

In Freeland there are five fundamental laws; and
of these the first is the most important; namely, that:
Every inhabitant has an equal right to the common
land and to the means of production which are furnished
by the state.

The other fundamental laws have to do with the support of women and children, old men, and those otherwise unfit to work, all of whom have the right of main-

tenance, corresponding to the amount of credit belonging to the state; with the provision of universal suffrage for all above twenty-five years of age; and with the establishment of independent legislative and executive branches of the government.

Let us follow the visitor to Freeland as he makes his first explorations in Edendale, its principal city, and learns how affairs are conducted. If this is an individualist utopia it is not by any means free from the services of a bureaucracy; for first of all the visitor turns to the Central Statistical Office, where records are kept of the occupations that are open and the amount of pay offered by each. "Every inhabitant of Freeland," our visitor finds, "has the right to become a member of any business he pleases. One has only to present oneself for this purpose; for the managers only decide upon the manner in which the members are to be employed, and not on the membership itself." In practice, the number of individuals with private businesses and partnerships seems to be limited, for big companies not merely operate factories but provide restaurant service, build houses, and even supply domestic service to private individuals and households.

(The visitor has his boots blacked by one of these associated menials, and his hostess explains how the services of a caterer and a valet may be obtained by calling up a central distributing agency.)

The sole condition upon which a person or company is allowed to engage in business is that the public be kept informed of all business transactions. "The companies are therefore obliged to conduct their bookkeeping openly. The prices at which goods are bought and sold, the net profits and the number of workmen, must be communicated at intervals which are fixed according to the judgment of the central office."

Observe that Hertzka reckons with the fact that in an industrial society, access to machinery is just as important as access to the land, since, in a manner of speaking, all our modern activities, even agriculture, are parasitic upon machinery. Hence the collection and distribution of capital is managed in the interests of the whole community; the first being taken care of by a yearly tax, which obviates the need—and perhaps the possibility—of individual savings, whilst the capital is distributed without interest to the companies that make application for it. The community pays for the plant through the added charge which is laid on consumers; the credit advanced is cancelled out through production. This arrangement does away with the standing charge for capital which is maintained under present day production for profit even after the original capital has been paid off in dividends; and above all, it does away with the practice of capitalizing increased returns in such a way as to enlarge the amount of the standing charge for capital. The social use of capital to advance production, rather than to provide fixed incomes for a rentier class, is recognized in Freeland.

Since our visitor is an engineer, he turns to a plant devoted to the manufacture of railway equipment; and notes that it is run under the following statutes.

1. Everyone is free to join the first Edendale Engine and Railway Manufacturing Co., even if he also belongs to other companies. Everyone is also permitted to leave the company whenever he chooses. The board of management decides in what branch of the works the members shall be employed.

[141]

2. Every member is entitled to an amount of the net proceeds of the company corresponding to the quantity of work which is done.

3. The amount of work is calculated according to the number of hours, to which two per cent. is added to that of the older members, and ten per cent. to foremen, and ten per cent. for night work.

4. The engineers are paid as if working from ten to fifteen hours, according to ability. The value of the manager is estimated in the general assembly.

5. Out of the company's profits a deduction is first made towards repayment of capital, and after this the tax to the state is deducted. The remainder is divided among members.

6. If the company is dissolved or liquidated, the members are responsible in proportion to the amount of profit which they get from revenues of the company, and this responsibility for the amount which is still pledged is proportionately laid upon new members. When a member leaves the company, his responsibility for debt which has already been contracted is not extinguished. In case of dissolution, liquidation, or sale, this responsibility corresponds to the claim of the responsible member to the means of the company which are in hand, or to his share in what is sold.

7. The principal judicial body of the company is the general assembly in which every member has the same right to speak and exercise the same active and passive right of choice. The general assembly makes its determination by simply counting the majority of votes. A majority of three quarters is necessary for changing the statutes and for a dissolution or liquidation of the company.

8. The general assembly practises its right either directly or by means of chosen officials, who are answerable to it for their actions.

9. The business of the society is managed by a directorate of three members who hold office at the will of the general assembly. The subordinate functionaries are chosen by the managers.

10. The general assembly selects every year a committee of inspection which consists of five members. This body has to control and make a report upon the books and the manner in which the company is conducted.

Now, as a member of the company, our visitor would have the amount he has earned credited to him at a Central Bank, which keeps his accounts and sends him an abstract every week; and through this bank he would make the larger part of his disbursements. The products of the company, moreover, are valued, stored, and sold by a Central Warehouse, in much the same fashion that under the present regime a manufacturer's whole output may be disposed of through a big department store or a mail order house.

Let us now sum this up. The collection and disposition of capital belongs to the community; and the total capital available for further production each year is based directly upon the productive capacities of the community, without the waste and leakage that arises in present-day society though what Mr. Thorstein Veblen calls the conspicuous waste—the futile expenditures—of the leisured classes. That this collection of a capital tax upon income would be any more difficult than the present corporation tax or private income tax, which is now dissipated to the extent of some 90 per

or so upon armies and navies, is seriously to be
ted. In addition to this, the process of open book-
eping enables the Central Bank and the Central
Warehouse to have an accurate knowledge of potential
production, and thus there exists an accurate basis for
apportioning credit. At the same time the value of
commodities comes by this means to have a direct relation to the costs of production rather than to what the
traffic will bear.

On all these heads the trained economist will doubtless have many points to contest; but in their broad
outlines there is no abrupt departure from current
practise in any of these items, and not much reason,
perhaps, why they should not be more thoroughly in-
stituted.

With the various ramifications of Edendale industry
and corporate finance it is not my business to deal;
we have gone far enough to see that very little indeed
remains when the question of means has been gone into.

The chief good that Freeland seems to offer is freedom in industrial enterprise. An association of men
can get land and capital on demand, and devote themselves to either agriculture or manufacturing industry;
and the risk of failure is minimized by a complete
knowledge of the probable demand and probable supply calculated by the statistical bureau. Failing an
outlet for industry through association, there remains
the land itself, for individual cultivation. "Every family in Freeland dwells in its own house, and every house
is surrounded by its great garden, a thousand square
meters in extent. These houses are the private property of the inhabitants, and serve, like the gardens,
for private use. The inhabitants of Freeland do not,

[144]

as a rule, recognize any kind of ownership of land; they rather go upon the principle that the land must be put in everyone's hands to do with what he chooses. This, in the most literal and wide sense of the word, means that every inhabitant of Freeland can cultivate every piece of land whenever he pleases. But this only relates to the land which is set apart for cultivation, and not that set apart for living upon. . . . The inhabitants of Freeland have agreed, with regard to the size and disposition of the land, serving for the creation of a dwelling house, to form regulations, and a kind of building court . . . which has to determine what ground is and what is not to be built upon, parcels out the land for building, sees to the laying out of streets, canals, and the like, and especially takes care that not more than one building is erected upon one building allotment."

5

What sort of life arises out of this kind of industrial association, these provisions for the common use of machinery and land? It is all rather dry and colorless, a sort of picture postcard view of the Promised Land.

We are told that there are a great number of public buildings in Edendale—an administrative palace, the Central bank, the University, the Academy of Arts, three Public Libraries, four Theaters, the grand central goods warehouse, a great number of schools and other buildings. In addition, extraordinary means are taken to provide for public cleanliness, and the aqueducts in Edendale—we seem to be reading a Chamber of Commerce report!—are "almost without any equal in the world," moreover, "they are being extended daily." The refuse is cleaned away by a system of pneumatic sucking apparatus. The streets are entirely macadamized. Electric tramways cross them in every direction and bind the suburbs to the town. Such glimpses as we get of Edendale remind us, in fact, of a go-ahead city in California or South Africa. The utopia of Freeland is progressive enough in all conscience; for many of these mechanical devices were only vague anticipations in 1889; but it is progressive in a mechanical sense; and when we examine it carefully, people seem to live the same sort of life here as they do in a "modern" European or American city.

There are differences, of course; and I do not seek to minimize their importance: the slum proletariat has been abolished; everyone belongs to the middle class and enjoys the felicities of a high-grade clerk or an engineer or minor official. This is the peculiarity of our nineteenth century utopians: they do not so much criticize the goods of their times as demand more of them! Buckingham and Hertzka, though they differ in details, wish to extend middle class values throughout society— comfort and security and a plenitude of soap and sanitation. Even when the means they propose are revolutionary, the institutions they would erect are conceived very much in the image of current use and wont, and are unspeakably tame.

As we pass from Hertzka to Bellamy these facts glare insistently at us. The slight air of tedium that I have not been able to disguise in dealing with these utopias arises, I believe, from our excessive familiarity with their contents. Our nineteenth century utopias, if we except those of Fourier and Spence and a few more

[146]

distinguished ones which we shall presently come to, do not dream of a renovated world: they keep on adding inventions to the present one. These utopias become vast reticulations of steel and redtape, until we feel that we are caught in the Nightmare of the Age of Machinery; and shall never escape. If this characterization seem unjust, I beg the reader to compare the utopias before Bacon with the utopias after Fourier, and find out how little human significance remains in the post-eighteenth century utopia when the machinery for supporting the good life is blotted out. These utopias are all machinery: the means has become the end, and the genuine problem of ends has been forgotten.

CHAPTER EIGHT

How Étienne Cabet dreamed of a new Napoleon called
Icar, and a new France called Icaria; and how his
utopia, with that which Edward Bellamy shows us
in Looking Backward, gives us a hint of what machinery might bring us to if the industrial organization were nationalized.

CHAPTER EIGHT

1

Étienne Cabet opened his eyes upon the year that preceded the meeting of the National Assembly in 1788, and closed them upon the Empire of Napoleon III. It would be foolish to give an account of Cabet's *Voyage en Icarie* without noting these facts; for the reason that Cabet's most impressionable years were drenched with the flamboyant light of the Napoleonic conquests and the Napoleonic tradition which remained as an afterglow when the conquests themselves had fallen below the horizon. The spectacle of a nationalized church and a nationalized system of education, extending their ministrations to the smallest commune through a vast system of bureaucracy, must have given a solidity to his dreams which the interruption of the first Napoleon's personal downfall could only have reinforced.

To understand why the Journey to Icaria, as we may call it, should have been one of the best sellers among workingmen in 1845, and to see why Louis Blanc should have attempted to set up an organization of National Workshops in 1848, one must realize the historic momentum of Napoleon's dictatorship. Cabet consciously or unconsciously idealized the Napoleonic tradition; and in Icaria he consummated it. That Cabet's futile will-to-power should have led him, under the inspiration of Owen, to the swamps of Missouri as

[151]

the leader of a little band of communist pioneers is an ironic twist of circumstance: his Icaria was a national state, with all its pomp and dignity and splendor, and not a squalid collection of huts in the midst of a dreary prairie. Cabet died in America, as much perhaps from an outraged sense of dignity as from any physical disease, and nothing came of his utopia until Edward Bellamy gave it a fresh outline in Looking Backward.

2

With the romantic element in the Journey to Icaria —the English lord and the Icarian family he visits, and the various friendships and love affairs that are outlined in its pages—I purpose to have nothing to do. These things add an element of complication to Cabet's picture without doing very much to illuminate it.

Icaria is a country divided into a hundred provinces almost equal in extent and almost the same in population. These provinces are in turn divided into ten communes, which are likewise almost equal, and the provincial capital is in the center of the province, whilst each communal city is the center of the commune. The elegance and precision of the decimal system has overlaid the facts of geography and as one looks over the map of the imaginary country one recalls the way in which the French revolution divided France into arbitrary administrative areas called departments, upsetting those ancient regional groupings which corresponded, roughly, with the natural units of soil, climate, population, and historic continuity.

In the midst of Icaria is the city of Icara. Icara is a reconstructed Paris, built on a reconstructed Seine.

It is almost circular, cut into two equal parts by a river whose banks have been straightened and enclosed in two straight walls; and the bed has been deepened to receive ocean vessels. In the middle of the city the river divides into two arms, which form a rather big circular island—though the islands formed naturally by the division of a river are inevitably not circular!—and here is the civic center, planted with trees, in the midst of which stands a palace. There is a superb garden elevated on a terrace; in the center, a vast column surmounted by a colossal statue that dominates all the buildings. On each side of the river is a big quay, bordered by public offices. The effect is indubitably metropolitan.

The city is divided into quarters: Icara has sixty communes of almost equal size. In each quarter is a school, a hospital, a temple, shops, public places, and monuments. The streets are straight and wide, the city being traversed by fifty avenues parallel to the river and fifty perpendicular to it. How it is possible to reconcile this street plan with a circular city I have no notion; and Cabet apparently did not take the trouble to cast his verbal specifications into a definite picture or plan. Each block has fifteen houses on each side, with a public building in the middle, and one at each end; and between the rows of houses are gardens which the inhabitants of Icaria, like those of Utopia, have a great pride in keeping up. The blocks are arranged around squares, very much like those of Belgravia and Mayfair in London; but the gardens are public ones and are cared for by the inhabitants.

The Icarian villages are almost as metropolitan as the principal city itself. One notes a great preoccupa-

[153]

tion with hygienic conveniences and sanitary regulations. There are dust collectors of special model; the sidewalks are covered with glass against rain; and the stations for omnibuses are also covered. The streets are well-lighted and paved. Stables, slaughter houses, and hospitals are on the outskirts of the village. The factories and warehouses are on the railway lines and canals, and half the streets are closed to all traffic except dog-carts.

In sum, Icaria enjoys a highly sophisticated and metropolitan form of life. Everything has been "arranged," everything has been "attended to." There are no upsetting complications and diversities. Even the weather has been disposed of. Nothing short of a very powerful and persistent organization could have accomplished these things. What is this organization?

3

In the beginning was Icar, the dictator who established the government of Icaria, and out of Icar there sprang a number of bureaux, departments, and committees. Let us follow a typical Icarian through his day, and examine the institutions he comes in contact with.

Our Icarian is an early riser by necessity, for at 6 A. M. breakfast is served in a restaurant or factory. It is not a capricious breakfast; it is such a breakfast, perhaps, as the guardians of Battle Creek, Michigan, dream of. The food that is served in Icaria is regulated by a committee of scientists; and while everybody has all that is good for him, precisely what is good and in what amounts, someone else has decided in advance.

[154]

So it is at present in our armies and navies, and to some extent in our cheap lunchrooms, the difference being that there remains, outside Icaria, the possibility of breaking away from the routine and following caprice and appetite without respect for the committee of dietitians.

When our Icarian has breakfasted, he goes to his work, seven hours in summer, six in winter. He works the same number of hours as every other Icarian, and whether he works in the field or the workshop, the products of his industry are deposited in public stores. Who is his employer? The State. Who owns all the instruments of production and service, down to the horses and carriages? The State. Who organizes the workers? The State. Who constructs the stores and factories, attends to the cultivation of the ground, has houses built, and makes all the things necessary for clothing, lodging, and transport? The same. In theory, the public is the sole proprietor and director of industry; in practice—Cabet doesn't tell us otherwise and it necessarily follows in a system of national industry—a body of engineers and officials have taken over the dictatorship of Icar and are running the affairs of the community.

How familiar this Icaria seems to us. Utopia—*c'est la guerre!*

When he is through with his work, our Icarian possibly changes his clothes. Exactly what clothes are necessary, and what are permissible has already been prescribed by a committee on clothes; which comes to saying that every Icarian's dress is a uniform, even as every Icarian is an official of the State. Eating, working, dressing, sleeping—there is no getting away from

State regulations. The uniformity that irks us in modern life and that makes people who have some remnant of free initiative in their makeup chafe in the civil service, to say nothing of the army, is extended to the last degree in Icaria. Napoleon's conception of a nation in arms is dominant; only now it is a nation in overalls.

Our Icarian's father and mother were married after a six-month interval of courtship. Since they took advantage of the institution at the earliest moment permitted by law, he was twenty and she was eighteen. By education, they had been taught to look upon conjugal fidelity as a desideratum; and they realized that concubinage and adultery would be looked upon as crimes by public opinion, even if these crimes were not punished by law. Before our Icarian was born his mother received public instruction on maternity.

Up to the age of five our Icarian's education was domestic; but from the fifth to the seventeenth or eighteenth year, domestic instruction was combined with intellectual and moral education, under a program laid down by a committee which had consulted all systems of education, ancient and modern. His general or elementary education was the same as that of every other Icarian; but at seventeen for girls and eighteen for men, his professional education began.

The only industries or professions open to our Icarians were those recognized and sanctioned by the State; and every year a list is published telling the number of workers needed in each profession. The number of workers, in turn, is determined by a committee on industry, which plans the amount of goods that must be produced during the coming year. Our

Icarian begins work at eighteen, his sister at seventeen; and he is exempt from work at sixty-five, while she would be exempt at fifty. The republic, I may note parenthetically, asks from each commune the sort of industrial and agricultural production which goes best with its natural resources; delivering its surplus production to other communes and giving it, in turn, what it may lack.

Cabet describes all these institutions in the minutest fashion, down to the noiseless window with which each Icarian's house is equipt; but the broad outlines of the industrial and social system are contained in this picture. What we see is a National State, abundantly organized for war, and remaining on that footing in the midst of its peace-time activities. What is not of national importance, in this scheme of things, is of no importance; and the people who decide what is or is not of national importance are the officeholders—I find it difficult to discover a utopian equivalent for this word or to fancy any great improvement in utopia—in the capital.

The political activities that regulate these Icarian institutions do not greatly reassure us. From each of the thousand communes two deputies are chosen to hold office for two years: this constitutes the national representation. The basis of this system is the communal assembly; and from this communal assembly the provincial representatives are drawn. The national executive consists of sixteen members, each with a special department; and it is plain that here is the seat of power; for exactly what business remains in the hands of the two thousand legislators when the food committee has determined the amount and variety of food, the

industrial committee the quantity and kind of manufactured products, and the educational committee the
methods, subjects, and aims of education, it is a little
hard to determine.

There are no newspapers and no means of organized
criticism, except the right of submitting propositions
to the popular assemblies. The only thing resembling
public opinion is the collective opinion of these assemblies. The newspapers are published by the government, one for the nation, one for the province, and one
for the commune; and they are devoted solely to the
presentation of news, divorced from opinion. For this
kind of political system, and for all the power that it
might presume to wield, there is a word in philosophy
which has no substitute—epiphenomenon. The popular
system of representation in Icaria is but a shadow of
that dictatorial power which was first wielded by Icar
and was in turn transmitted to the committees and
bureaux.

If I have been criticizing Icaria in terms of the last
century of political experience, I can only plead that
it is because Icaria is so little like Utopia and so much
like the actual order of things. It must be prepared
to stand fire as a *fait accompli:* indeed, in the early days
of the second Russian revolution it came near to being
a *fait accompli*—there was more of Cabet than of
Marx perhaps in embryonic Soviet Russia! Icaria is
essentially not an ideal but an idealization; and it is
in order to keep the two from being confused that I
have emphasized its little weaknesses. What is good
in Icaria is what is good in the institution of an army;
what is bad is what is bad in the execution of a war.
If the good life could be perpetrated by a junta of

busybodies, as Plato would call them, Icaria would be a model community.

4

Looking backward into the future: that was the paradox by which a young New England romancer, Edward Bellamy, concerned like Thoreau and Emerson and the rest of the great Concord school with the well-being of his community, descended from literature to sociology; and stirred the minds of thousands of people in America in much the same fashion that Theodor Hertzka, writing at the same time, stirred his European contemporaries. Having begun to romanticize about reality, Bellamy during the decade that followed the publication of Looking Backward, devoted himself to realizing his romance. In a later work, Equality, he set forth his picture of the New Society of the year 2000 in much greater detail; just as if the popularity of his first work committed him to take up seriously the tasks of the economist and the statesman.

The chief pleasure, nowadays, in both of these books is the familiar one of recognition; for if Bellamy did not portray a better future he at any rate, like Mr. H. G. Wells, in his early romances, outlined many parts of a future that has for us, in the twentieth century, become an actuality; a fact which makes us realize very poignantly the limitations of his utopia. In spite of a thin-lipped style, Bellamy handles his story in a neat, workmanlike way, with a certain plausibility and familiarity which doubtless explains the fact that it can still be found, without any difficulty, on the fiction shelves of our circulating public libraries.

The preface to Looking Backward is dated: "Historical Section Shawmut College, Boston, December 26, 2000." In that preface the work is presented as an avowed romance which will enable the readers of 2000 to realize the gaps that separate them from their ancestors, and to value the prodigious "moral and material" transformation that has taken place in a few, generations. Julius West is a person whom our Shawmut historian invents, to bridge the gap between the two eras, Julius West, a young man of wealth, sensitive to the ignominy of his position, and feeling that, as a "rich man living among the poor, an educated man among the uneducated," he "was like one living in isolation among a jealous and alien race." In order to overcome his insomnia West sleeps in a vaulted room in the foundations of his house, and gets put to sleep by a hypnotist; and so by a dramatic oversight he hibernates for 113 years, and awakens among strange faces. Needless to say, West has a love affair in the old world which is carried on in the new, through a descendant of the girl he meant to marry; and it is equally needless to observe that he reawakens to the world of 1887 as soon as the institutions of 2000 have been described and the love affair has been resolved.

Let us take West's muzziness, his amazement, and his sense of isolation for granted, and follow him as he explores his new environment.

5

If Plato cavalierly disposes of the labor problem of the Republic by permitting things to remain pretty much as they were, Bellamy makes the solution of labor organization and the distribution of wealth the key to every other institution in his utopia.

In the United States of 1887 the growing organization of labor and the aggregation of capital into trusts were the two chief economic factors: Dr. Leete, Julius West's host, pictures how this aggregation and combination were continued until, by a mere shift of gears, "the epoch of trusts had ended in The Great Trust." In a word, "the people of the United States concluded to assume the conduct of their own business, just as one hundred years before they had assumed the conduct of their own government, organizing now for industrial purposes on precisely the same grounds that they had organized for political purposes." Was there any violence in this transition? Ah no! everything had been prepared beforehand by public opinion, the great corporations had gradually trained everybody into an acceptance of large-scale organization, and the final step of merging all the big corporations into a national corporation occurred without a jar. With the assumption by the nation of the mills, machinery, railroads, farms, mines, and capital in general, all the difficulties of labor vanished, for every citizen became by virtue of his citizenship an employee of the government, and was distributed according to the needs of industry.

In 2000 "the labor army" is not a figure of speech: it is an army indeed, for the nation is a single industrial unit, and the principle upon which the working force is recruited is universal compulsory industrial service. After a man's education has been completed in the common school system, which extends straight through college, he must first serve a term of three

[161]

years in an unclassified labor army, which performs all the rough and menial tasks of the community. When this period is over, he is permitted to offer himself as a recruit in any of the trades or professions which may be declared open by the government, and can train for his calling up to the age of thirty, in the national schools and institutes. In order to attract people into occupations where they are needed, the hours are reduced and, for the dangerous trades, volunteers are called for. There are however no discriminations in pay. Every person is credited with a sum of four thousand dollars per annum at the National Bank, a sum which he receives because of his needs as a man and not because of his capacity as a worker. Instead of being rewarded for giving the full measure of his energies and abilities, a man is penalized if he fails to do so. It is possible to shift from one branch of the service to another, under certain restrictions, even as in the navy one can change one's rating and apply for service on a different ship or station, but except for the possibility of retiring on a half-income at the age of thirty-three, everyone must remain at work until he is forty-five.

To this rule there is one exception; and we may note ironically that it is made in favor of the writer's guild. If a man produces a book he may name his own royalties, and live as long from this income as the sale will allow; and if he wishes to start a newspaper or a magazine, and can get credit from a sufficient number of other people to support his enterprise, there is nothing to prevent him from remitting service to the amount his guarantors are ready to deduct from their personal income. In other words, a man must "either by literary, artistic, or inventive productiveness indemnify the nation for the loss of his services, or must get a sufficient number of people to contribute to such an indemnity." This is the one open hole in our militarized, industrial utopia; and I think it is the most acceptable feature in the whole system. A community organized as a single unit, directed by a general staff at Washington, and perpetually exhibiting a herd complex which every institution would naturally reinforce, might not be a very genial shelter for the soul of an artist; but if it were, this means of support would doubtless be fair and excellent for the encouragement of the arts.

To go back to our army. The entire field of production and distribution is divided into ten great departments, each representing a group of allied industries; and each particular industry is in turn represented by a subordinate bureau, which has a complete record of the plant and the force under its control, of the present product, and of the means of increasing it. The estimates of the distributive department, after adoption by the administration, are sent as mandates to the ten great departments, which allot them to the subordinate bureaux, representing the particular industries, and these set the men at work. . . . "After the necessary contingents have been detailed for the various industries, the amount of labor left for other employment is expended in creating fixed capital, such as buildings, machinery, engineering works, and so forth."

In order to safeguard the consumer from the caprices of the administration, a new article must be produced as soon as a certain guaranteed demand for it has been established by popular petition, whilst an old article must be continued to be produced as long as there are customers for it, provision being made that the price rise in accordance with the greater cost of production per unit.

Now the general of this industrial army is the president of the United States. He is chosen from among the corps commanders; and it is provided that every officer in the army, from the president down to the sergeant, must work his way up from the grade of common laborer. The chief peculiarity of this system consists in the way in which the voting is done. The voters are all honorary members of the guild to which they belong; that is, men who are over forty-five years old; this applies not merely to the ten lieutenant generals, but to the commander-in-chief, who is not eligible for the presidency until he has been a certain number of years out of office. The president is elected by vote of all the men of the nation who are not connected with the industrial army; for any other method, Bellamy thinks, would be prejudicial to discipline. There are various names for this practice: one of them is gerontocracy, or government by the aged; and another, more familiar, is "alumni control." When we recollect that the hardships of military service look rather mild and pleasant to the man who has been mustered out, I doubt if the youngsters in the industrial army would stand much chance of having their lot improved if the initiative for a change had to come from the alumni. Yet we know what even the formation of a worker's shop committee would be in an industrial army: it would be mutiny. As for criticism of the administration, that would be treason; admiration for the practices of another country would be disloyalty; and advocacy of a change in the method of industry would be sedition.

[164]

True: corruption and bribe-taking and all the dirty
scandals that we associate today with a financial oli-
garchy would be wiped out in utopia; but this merely
means that the defects of the old order would disappear
along with its virtues. What would remain would be
the defects that arise when a nation is in arms, and
when there is no escape, by travel or mental withdrawal,
from its institutions; in short, the defects of a state
of war. To call this a peaceful community is absurd:
one might as well call a battleship a pleasure-craft because a modern one possesses a band and shows motion
pictures to the crew. The organization of this utopia
is an organization for war; and the one rule that such
a community would not tolerate is "live and let live."
If this is the peace that "industrial preparedness"
ensures it is scarcely worth having. Any community
that liked this state of life would scarcely need the
constant exhortation of the recruiting sergeant or the
final compulsion of a conscription act.

6

The great part of Looking Backward is a discussion
of this perfected form of industrial organization; the
manner in which it is worked; and the effects of complete economic equality in doing away with the necessity
for the greater part of the legal machinery of the present day, since crimes with an economic motive would
almost, according to Bellamy, be unthinkable. Here
and there however we have glimpses of the social life of
this new age.

First of all, there floats before our eyes the picture
of a vast body of superannuated persons, who for the

[165]

most part spend their time in a sort of country-club existence. They can travel, because the other countries in the world are likewise nationalized, and by a simple system of book-keeping foreign credit for goods and personal services can be transferred from one country to another; and they can take up special vocations and hobbies during their superannuated years; but it is equally plain that their work has not done very much to foster intellectual or emotional maturity, since in relation to the citizens the state exists as a "Great White Father"; and there is good reason perhaps for the great interest in sport which characterizes Bellamy's utopia. Games are organized, apparently, upon lines of industrial guild rivalry; just as one has sports nowadays between rival battleship squadrons perhaps; for "if bread is the first necessity of life, recreation is a second, and the nation caters for both." The demand for bread and circuses, our guide explains, is recognized in the year 2000 as a wholly reasonable one. Both work and play are external to the citizen's inner trends and interests; and we should not be surprised if an infantile element predominated in the character of this happy republic.

This externalism, this impersonality, seems to characterize the whole scene. We follow Julius West and his new love, Edith, into a modern shop, where everything is displayed by sample, and an order for goods is sent to a central warehouse, and along with undoubted economies of space and time, we note that there is an almost complete absence of personal contacts or relationships: more than ever the worker has become a cog in the machine, more than ever he deals with a thin, barren, abstract world of paper notations, more

than ever his desire for social contacts is dammed
up; and so, more than ever, there must be occasion in
this new age for stimulants and socialities beside which
the roller coasters of Coney Island and the promiscui-
ties of a modern dance hall would be insipid things.
Bellamy does not show us what these compensatory institutions would be: but he has invented a high-powered
engine of repression, and he does not fool us when he con-
ceals the safety-valve. Unless there is a safety-valve his
universal army, under a rigorous discipline for twenty-
four years, is bound to blow up the works. We can guess
when we read the cheap illustrated papers, when we go
to the movies, when we watch the behavior of the crowds
on Broadway, what this twenty-first century Utopia
would be like—it would be all that a modern city is,
exaggerated. In The New Society, Dr. Walter Rath-
enau drew a picture of a socialized modern society,
moving along its present path without any change in
its aims and ideals; and that nightmare of his must be
added to Bellamy's dream in order to define it.

It is the same with every other institution. There
is a big communal restaurant in which each family of
the neighborhood has a private room; this is the place
where the principal meal is ordered by the family, and
served by young conscript waiters. Am I at fault if
I point out that this universal hostelry is a little too
elaborate and mechanical; that there is more promise of
a genuine utopia in Plato's olives and cheese and beans,
simply served, than in the "perfection of catering and
cooking" which the new age boasts. So one could go
down the line and enumerate the mechanical marvels
which take the place of a fully humanized life; marvels
like the telephone concerts and sermons which astound-

ingly anticipate by thirty-odd years the radio broad-
casting service which is now a prevalent mania in
America. Are these things, as Aristotle would have
said, the material bases of the good life, or are they
substitutes for the good life? There may have been
some doubt as to the answer in Bellamy's time; but
I think there need not be any at present. In so far as
these instruments are consonant with humanized purposes they are good; in so far as they are irrelevant
they are so much rubbish—idiotic rubbish. A free
public library is a good thing; but a free public library
devoted exclusively to distributing the novels of Gene
Stratton Porter and the uplift books of Mr. Orison
Swett Marden would not contribute so much as a useful platitude towards a vivid and stimulating society.

There is no escaping the problem of ends and the
problem of ends, if I may be permitted a pun, belongs
at the beginning. Subordinate to humanized ends, machinery and organization—yes, complicated machinery
and organization—have undoubtedly a useful contribution to make towards a good community; unsubordi-
nated, or subordinated only to the engineer's conceptions of an efficient industrial equipment and personnel,
the most innocent machine may be as humanly devastating as a Lewis gun. All this Bellamy overlooked in
Looking Backward, and yet—something remains.

What remains in Looking Backward is the honest
passion that inspired the man; the play of generous
impulses; the insistence that there is no fun for an
ordinarily imaginative person in dining with Dives
whilst Lazarus hangs around the table. Bellamy
wanted everyone to be equally educated, so that everyone might be his companion; he wanted everyone to be

decently fed and sheltered; he wanted to take his share
in the dirty work and to see that accidents of wealth
did not keep other people from taking theirs. He
wanted private life to be simple and public life to
be splendid. He wanted men and women to mate with
each other without permitting this relationship to be
compromised by obligations to a father, a mother, or the
butcher, the baker, and the grocer. He wanted the
generous, the just, and the tender-hearted to be as well
endowed as the cold-hearted, the greedy, and the self-
seeking. He pleaded for an absence of artificiality and
restraint in the relations of the sexes; for such a candor as has perhaps come into fashion again—thank
heaven!—today, a candor which permits women physical freedom in dress, and a spiritual freedom in exhibiting their love, and giving it freely. All this is to
the good. I do not question Bellamy's fine motives;
I question only the outlets he imagined for them. There
is a breach between Bellamy's conception of the good
life and the structure he erected to shelter it. This
breach is due, I believe, to an over-emphasis of the part
that wholesale mechanical organization, directed by a
handful of people, would play in such a reconstruction.
If Bellamy sometimes exaggerated the bad in modern
society, with its muddle of competitive privileges, he
likewise overestimated the good that it contained; and
he was more than fair to the present order of things
when he made the future so closely in its image.

CHAPTER NINE

How William Morris and W. H. Hudson renew the
classic tradition of utopias; and how, finally, Mr.
H. G. Wells sums up and clarifies the utopias of
the past, and brings them into contact with the
world of the present.

CHAPTER NINE

1

It would be a pretty sad thing if the Utopias of the nineteenth century were all of a piece with those of Buckingham and Bellamy. In general we may say that all the utopias of reconstruction had a deadly sameness of purpose and a depressing singleness of interest; and although they saw society whole, they saw the problem of reconstructing society as a simple problem of industrial reorganization. Fortunately, the utopias of escape have something to contribute which the utopias of reconstruction lack; and if William Morris, for example, seems too remote from Manchester and Minneapolis to be of any use, he is by that token a little nearer the essential human realities: he knows that the chief dignity of man lies not in what he consumes but in what he creates, and that the Manchester ideal is—devastatingly consumptive.

Before I go into these utopias of escape, I wish to point out the strange way in which the three utopias we shall examine return as it were upon their classic models, each of the returns being, it is fairly plain, without the consciousness of the writer. Mr. W. H. Hudson returns upon More; and in A Crystal Age the farmstead and the family is the ultimate unit of social life. In News from Nowhere the city of workers, such as Andreæ dreamed of, comes again into being; and in A Modern Utopia, with its order of Samurai, we are ruled once more by a highly disciplined class of Platonic guardians. Mr. Hudson is a naturalist with a deep sympathy for the rural life of England; William Morris was a craftsman who knew what the English town was like before it had been blighted by industrialism; and with both of these men we feel close to the essential life of man and the essential occupations.

2

As the clouded vision of the traveller to the Crystal Age clears, he finds himself received in a great Country House, which is inhabited by a large group of men and women who till the land and perform the simple operations of weaving and stonecutting and the like. All over the world, one gathers, these great country houses dot the landscape. Each of them is no week-end center of social life but a permanent home; indeed their permanence is almost past believing; for in each house traditions are carried back thousands of years. The great cities and the complicated metropolitan customs that they produced have long been wiped away, as one might wipe away mold. The world has been stabilized; the itch for getting and spending has disappeared. Our traveller must bind himself to work for a whole year in order to pay for the garments his house-mates weave for him, garments whose texture and cut have a classic turn.

This household, I say, is the social unit of the Crystal Age: the house-father administers the laws and customs, and he dispenses the punishment of seclusion when the visitor trespasses upon the code of the house. The house-mates work together, eat together, play to-

[174]

gether, and listen together to the music of a mechanical instrument called the musical sphere. At night they sleep in separate little cubicles which can be opened to the night air. The horses and dogs of the Crystal Age have a degree of intelligence which our common breeds do not possess, so that the horses all but harness themselves to the plow, and the dog teaches the traveller when to leave off working the animals. Each household has not merely its laws and traditions: it has its literature; its written history; and the very girl with whom the traveller falls in love bears a resemblance to the sculptured face of an unhappy house-mother who lived and suffered in the immemorial past. These houses, these families, these social relations are built for endurance. What is the secret of their strength?

The secret of our Crystal Age Utopia is the secret of the beehive: a queen bee. The Crystallites have done away with the difficulties of mating by appointing one woman, in every house, to be the house-mother, the woman whose capital duty is to carry on the family: the entire burden of each generation falls upon her shoulders, and in return for the sacrifice she is treated with the respect due to divinity, like the young man who was chosen in the Kingdom of Montezuma, as the tales have it, to represent the chief deity until at the end of a year he was disembowelled. The wish of a house-mother is a command; the word of the house-mother is law. For a year before her retirement as mother she is put into communion with the sacred books of the house, and has at her command a store of knowledge which the rest of the hive are not permitted to share. It is she who keeps burning the fires of life.

For all except the house-mother sex is a matter of

purely physical appearance. The Crystallites, if
we may speak irreverently, are "content with a
vegetable love—which would certainly not suit me" nor,
it appears, did it suit our traveller to the Crystal Age,
when he discovers that his passion could never be re-
ciprocated by his beloved, even if she so far trans-
gressed the laws of the household as to give way to him.
Against the appearance of passion and all the mortal
griefs that it carries with it, the house-mother possesses a remedy. When in the murk of despair our
traveller turns to her for advice and consolation, she
gives him a phial of liquid. He drinks it in the belief
that it will make him as free from passion as his house-
mates; and he is not deceived; for—he dies.

The social life of the household is not to be wrecked
by the storms and stresses of the individual's passions.
The engines of life are no longer dangerous: the fuel
has been taken away! A "chill moonlight felicity" is
all that remains.

3

There are times when one may look upon the whole
adventure of civilized life as a sort of Odyssey of domes-
tication; and in this mood the Crystal Age marks a
terminus upon that particular aspect of the adventure.
To the objection that this sort of utopia requires that
we change human nature, the answer, in terms of modern biology, is that there is no apparent scientific
reason why certain elements in human nature should
not be selected and brought to the front, or why certain others should not be reduced in importance and
eliminated. So, for all practical purposes, there is no
apparent reason why human nature should not be

changed, or why we should not be prepared to believe
that in times past it has been changed—communities
which selectively bred for pugnacity and aggression
committing suicide and opening the way for communities which socially selected other traits that made for
survival. It is possible that in times past man has
done a great deal to domesticate himself and fit himself
for harmonious social life; and a utopia which rests
upon the notion that there should be a certain direction
in our breeding is not altogether luny; indeed, is nowadays less so than ever before, for the reason that it is
possible to separate romantic love from physical pro-
creation without, as the Athenians did, resorting to
homosexuality.

If A Crystal Age opens our minds to these possibilities it is not to be counted purely as a romance;
in spite of the fact that as a romance it has passages
that rival Green Mansions. Between the individual
households and common marriages, the utopia of the
beehive is a third alternative which possibly remains to
be explored.

4

There are regions in the world—I am thinking perhaps of the table land of South Africa and the Mis-
sissippi Valley—where if one dreamed about utopia the
apparatus to support it would be a gigantic network of
steel, and huge communities of people would naturally
flow together and coalesce in complicated patterns,
somewhat after the fashion of those which Mr. H. G.
Wells describes in When the Sleeper Awakens. It
would be almost impossible, I fancy, to dream of a simple life and of handfuls of people in those parts of the

[177]

earth: the simplicity would be barrenness, and a handful of people would be lost.

It is different with the valley of the Thames, that little stream which begins a short way above Oxford and meanders between banks of lush grass and bending willows, down through Marlow, where musty ales have long been made, past Windsor between the Great Park and the Chiltern Hills, through Richmond and so down to Hammersmith where one might perhaps ford the river at low tide if an iron bridge did not carry one across, till below the city of London the estuary becomes a wide tide of water and expands proudly to meet the sea. Nature has carved this valley to the human scale: the houses are not dwarfed by the landscape; and except for the huge warren of London—for which nature is not responsible—there is a fitness between the actor and the scene which, without offering any great Olympian moments, gives the naïve and jolly and wholehearted effect that one finds in a good English hunting print or, let us say, in Pickwick Papers. In such an atmosphere, particularly as one thinks of it on a day late in June, human nature bubbles naturally into good nature, and whatever harshness remains, a tankard of ale will drain away.

It is in this valley of the Thames that William Morris awoke to find his utopia, after returning to his home in Hammersmith, the last really urban borough of London as one goes upstream. From that landscape, sweetened and freshened and ridden of cockney landmarks, Morris evokes the spirit of the River God, as Socrates and Phædrus, by the banks of the Ilyssus, call forth the spirit of Pan.

With all the grime and tedium of the dull 'eighties

lying upon his soul, Morris finds himself transported
to a world which has been cleansed by a revolution of
a greater part of the nineteenth century landmarks.
In the meanwhile, grass has laid a decent blanket over
many irretrievable ruins. The house in which he has
gone to bed is now a Guest House; and he is first received into this refurbished world by a boatman who
takes him for a morning swim on the Thames, and
knows about the value of money only as a collector of
copper curios might. At breakfast, he finds himself
among a group of friendly people, who call him "Guest";
and he is taken firmly and sweetly and quite serenely
in hand by the comely young women who preside over
the house. These women, like everyone else in the new
Thames valley, are healthy, full-blooded, athletic, sane,
and free from the puling maladies which idleness or
overwork gave to the women of the nineteenth century. The other guests are a weaver who has come
down from the north to take a turn at the boatman's
job while the latter goes up towards Oxford to help
gather in the hay, and a loquacious dustman in marvel-
lous greens and golds.

In this new England, work has become what one
would call in the kindergarten "busy work": in the sim-
plification of the standard of living and the release from
the pressure of artificially stimulated wants, the main
business of getting a living is easily performed, and
the chief concern of everyone is to do his work under
the pleasantest conditions possible—a demand which
brings back many of the handicrafts, and places a great
premium on manual skill. Although the mechanical
arts have been improved in certain directions, for in his
trip up the Thames our guest meets with a barge

driven by some internal engine, let us say by electricity, a good many devices have been allowed to fall into disuse, because, although the output in goods might be greater, the work itself and the way of life it promotes are not so beneficial as the simple methods of hand labor. In every direction, simplicity and direct action and the immediate supply and interchange of goods out of local produce, has taken the place of the monstrously complicated system of traffic that prevailed in the earlier imperialistic world. Work is given freely, and the proceeds of work exchanged freely, as a man might give of his goods and services nowadays when he welcomes a friend within his own house. A great part of the energy of this new community has gone into building; and architecture, sculpture, and painting flourish in the townhalls and common dining halls of which each village boasts.

It follows from this that the big cities have disappeared. London is again a congeries of villages, mingled in great woodlands and meadows where in the summer children roam about and camp and pick up the simple occupations of rural life. Of all the proud monuments of London that the nineteenth century left, only the Houses of Parliament remain, as a storage-place for dung. There are shops, where one takes for the asking, and there are common halls where people eat and have conversation, as they do now in restaurants—only these new hostels are beautiful, spacious, and well-served.

Since economic pressure is absent, the people of the Thames valley seem to live a life of leisure; but this life of leisure is not the aimless leisure of the country house, with its artificial stimulants, its artificial exercises, and the like: the life of dignified leisure is a life of work; in short, the life of the artist. If other people have talked of the necessity for labor, the dignity of labor, the heroism of labor, these simple Englishmen have discovered the beauty of leisurely work— the simple grace that follows when even the practical arts are pursued as if they were liberal arts. In this utopia the instinct of workmanship, the creative impulse, has free play; and since the majority of people are neither scholars nor scientists, as Sir Thomas More would have had them, they find their fulfillment in adding beauty to all the necessities of their daily toil. Where the work itself leads purely to some useful end, as in the growing of wheat or grass, the joy of work arises out of the comradeship and good-feeling that bind together those who perform it, and the comparative lightness of the tasks that find many hands eager almost to the point of competition to perform them.

One looks at the faces of these people, and the effects of their life are visible. Their women are ten or fifteen years older than we should judge by their appearance; and on every face is written the healthy serenity that follows when people do good work, with a good spirit, in a good place. There is a candor, a plainness, a wholesomeness, an absence of furtive repressions in their every gesture; and as far as men can be satisfied and happy in a good environment, this community is satisfied and happy. There are grumblers, it goes without saying. One of them is a crusty old fellow who has read ancient history and who sighs for the cutthroat practices of the competitive era; and there is another who complains of the tameness of Utopian literature, as compared with that which dealt with the miseries and warped passion of an earlier age.

The only wretchedness in this utopia comes out of the essential human tragedy—the disparity between one's aims and one's attainments, between one's desires and the circumstances that clog their fulfillment. How can unhappiness be altogether wiped out as long as maids are fickle and sexual passion strong? The boatman, for example, has been mated with a beautiful girl who leaves him for another man; but she tires of her new love, and under the eyes of the Guest her uncle brings the pair together, and the drama of courtship and mating goes on all over again; for there are no laws to bind people together when every fibre of their being drives them apart; and in a civilization that deals kindly even with its adults there is no difficulty about giving the children all the care they need. For the most part, those who suffer in love bear their burdens manfully, without wailing over imaginary wrongs which are associated with the worship of impossible chastities and reticences; and they turn their balked impulses into the channels of work and poetry as completely as they know how.

Is this the arcadian age of innocence all over again? Are brutality and lust forever wiped out? Not at all. In sudden passion even murders occur, no matter how good and helpful the social order; but instead of compounding murder with an additional murder, the guilty person is left to his own remorse. Use and wont are more powerful than law, and the whole guild that earns its living from the frictions and dissidences of our social life has dropt into limbo. By the same token, the game of the ins and the outs, which we

[182]

call political government, has disappeared; for the only matters in which our community is interested are as to whether a new field is to be laid under the plow or a bridge thrown over a stream or a townhall built; and about such things the local community is competent to decide, without lining up in a purely fictitious antagonism.

5

Sanity and health and good-will and tolerance—as one sculls along the Thames, above Richmond, on a Sunday morning, between boatloads of gay picnickers and sauntering people, it is not impossible to imagine a new social order developing on simple lines and bringing these things into existence. With five million people in England, and perhaps half a million in the Thames valley, the thing would not be impossible. Then the whole countryside would be dressed again in green; then buildings would arise in the landscape like flowers out of the ground; then the kindliness and spontaneous co-operation of a happy holiday would be prolonged into the workaday week. We should know how to spend our time and with what to occupy our heads and hands, if the great wen of London were removed from the Thames valley, and all the cheap cockney things that London has conjured into existence were to be blasted away. We should know all these things, because William Morris has told us about them; and we should do all these things, because in our heart of hearts we realize that they would satisfy.

6

The utopia that remains for consideration is the last important one in point of time; and it is, curiously

[183]

enough, the quintessential utopia, for it is written with a free and critical gesture, and with a succinct familiarity towards the more important books that came before it. Mr. H. G. Wells, it is true, has made more than one excursion into an imaginary commonwealth: The Time Machine is his earliest and The World Set Free may possibly be considered as his latest. A Modern Utopia combines the vivid fantasy of the first picture with the more strict regard for present realities that marks the second; and it is, altogether, a fine and lucid product of the imagination.

The assumption upon which Mr. Wells gains entrance into his utopia differs from those shipwrecks and somnambulisms in which our modern utopias have been stereotyped. He conceives of a modern man, a little thickset and protuberant, seated at a desk and brooding over the possibilities of man's future; and gradually this image comes to life and defines his views, and his voice rises into narrative in something like the fashion of a lecturer, throwing from time to time his illustrations of a New World upon the screen. He enters utopia by hypothesis; that is, without any other subterfuge than an act of the imagination; and in the thickening realities of a utopian community, first discovered in an Alpine pass, he finds himself in the company of a sentimental botanist, who is sick with a love affair and is maudlin about dogs, and who again and again wrecks this exploration of utopia by dragging into the midst of the scene some petty complication—about his sweetheart or his doggie—that he has acquired on earth!

Where and what is this modern utopia? By hypothesis, it is a globe identical with the one on which we

live; it has the same oceans and continents, the same
rivers and minor land-masses, the same animals and
plants; yes, even the same people, so that each one of
us has his utopian counterpart. Conveniently, this new
earth is located beyond Sirius; and for the most part
its history is parallel to ours; except that it had a
critical turn for the better at a not too remote period;
so that, while mechanical invention and science and
all that sort of thing is exactly on the same level as
ours, the scale and order is entirely different.

The scale and order of things is indeed different.
Utopia is a world community; it is a single civilization whose net of monorails and posts, whose identifica-
tion bureaux, whose rules of law and order are the same
in England as in Switzerland; and presumably the
same in Asia and Africa as in Europe. In every sense
it is a modern utopia. Machinery plays an important
part, and the absence of menial service is conspicuous
from the very first contacts in which our travellers get
the hospitality of an inn, and find that interior decoration has verged towards the style of the modern lunch-
room and subway station, so that the whole room can be
redded, after use, by the guest himself. There is no
harking back to the past in industry, in architecture, or
in the mode of living. All that machinery has to offer
has been accepted and humanized: there is a cleanliness,
an absence of squalor and confusion, in this world-
community, which indicates that utopia has not been
purchased by evasion.

The price of this order and spaciousness is not as
heavy as that which Bellamy was willing to pay in
Looking Backward. The land and its natural resources
are owned by the community and are in the custody of

regional authorities; and the means of communication and travel are in the hands of one common administrative body. There are great socialized enterprises such as the railways, with planetary ramifications; there are regional industries, and there are a good many minor affairs which are still undertaken by private individuals and companies. Farms are worked by a co-operative association of tenant farmers, upon lines suggested by Dr. Hertzka in Freeland. Perhaps the most remarkable feature of utopian organization is the registration of every individual, with his name, numeral, finger-print, changes of residence and changes in life; all of which is filed in a huge central filing office, to become part of a permanent file upon the individual's death. Utopian registration gets our travellers into hot water, for they are naturally mistaken for their utopian doubles; but outside of its use in the story this little device seems strangely beside the point, and it arose, I believe, out of Mr. Wells' temperamental regard for tidiness— tidiness on a planetary scale—the tagging and labelling of a well-conducted shop. . . .

The people of our Modern Utopia are roughly divided into four classes: the kinetic, the poietic, the base, and the dull. The kinetic are the active and organizing elements in the community: as active kinetics they are the managers, the enterprisers, the great administrators, as passive kinetics they are the minor officials, the innkeepers, the shoptenders, farmers, and the like. The poietic are the creative elements in the community; the "intellectuals" we should perhaps call them. This follows in general the lines laid down by Comte—chiefs. people, intellectuals, and emotionals, and perhaps something of the same classification was outlined by More

[186]

in his Philarchs, people, priests, and scholars. This division of classes is a very ancient one. In that old Indian script, the Bhagavad Gita, we find that the population is divided into Brahmans, Kshatriyas, Vaisryas, and Sudras, and that their duties are "determined by the modes that prevail in their separate natures." The residual classes of the base and the dull correspond to the Sudras; they are, of course, the slag of the community; and the active elements in this class, the criminals, the habitual drunkards, and the like are exported to various islands in the Atlantic where they have organized a community of their own in which they may practice fraud, chicane, and violence to their hearts' content.

Like Plato, Mr. Wells is concerned to provide for the education, discipline, and maintenance of people who will be sufficiently disinterested and intelligent to keep this vast organization a going concern—no ordinary politician or captain of industry will do. Hence there arises a class of Samurai. These Samurai are selected by rigorous mental and physical tests out of youth who are past twenty-five, up to which time they may be foolish and unsettled and may sow their wild oats. These Samurai have a high intellectual standard of achievement. They live a simple life. They are under strict moral discipline, and follow a minute regimentation of dress and minor details of conduct. They cannot marry out of their class. Once a year they are sent out into the forests, the mountains, or the waste places to shift for themselves; they go "bookless and weaponless, without pen or paper, or money"; and they come back again with a new hardness and fineness and fortification of spirit. It is such an organization as might

[187]

have been evolved at the time of the Reformation had
the Order of Jesuits been able to effect a dictatorship
of Christendom. I say this without disparagement of
either the Jesuits or the Samurai, in order to point
out that these guardians of A Modern Utopia are plau-
sible historic characters. All the important economic
and political enterprises of the state, and important
vocations like that of the physician, are in the hands of
Samurai. They are as necessary to the social organization of A Modern Utopia as the research laboratories,
which are provided by charter with each factory, are
necessary to its industrial organization.

7

The glimpses that one gets of this utopia are full of
color and light and movement; there are finely contained
cities, surrounded by wide suburban territories, cities
that are not built of paper and alabaster. Lovers
pass arm in arm through the streets in the twilight;
and there is a soft dignity in the women, with their
gay, sexually unemphatic dresses, that charms. There
are electric trains weaving silently on rails over the
landscape of Europe, crossing under the English Chan-
nel by tube, and emerging in London with none of the
bustle, the grinding, or the dirt of a modern railway
ride. There are well-cultivated fields and adequate
inns. There are no obstreperous patriotisms, as one
suspects in Looking Backward; there is none of the
shirking one might fear in News from Nowhere. (While
our travellers are waiting to be identified they stay
for a while in a residential quadrangle at Lucerne, and
are given employment in a toy workshop.) There is
less dogmatism about creeds than in Christianopolis,

[188]

and an entire absence of menialism which contrasts with More's Utopia.

This modern utopia brings together, compares, and criticizes important points that all the other utopias have raised; and it does all this with a deftness and a turn of humor that speaks for Mr. Wells at his best. Above all, A Modern Utopia strikes a new note, the note of reality, the note of the daily world from which we endeavor in vain to escape. More or less, all the other utopias assume that a change has come over the population; that it has been diminished; that the blind, the lame, and the deaf have been cured; that the mean sensual man has been converted and is ready to flap his wings and sing Hallelujah! There is a minimum of these assumptions in A Modern Utopia. It is above all other things an accounting and a criticism; and so it forms a fitting prelude to the remainder of this book.

CHAPTER TEN

How the Country House and Coketown became the
utopias of the Modern Age; and how they made
the world over in their image.

CHAPTER TEN

1

Now that we have ransacked the literature of ideal commonwealths for examples of the utopian vision and the utopian method, there remains another class of utopias which has still to be reckoned with, in order to make our tally complete.

All the utopias that we have dealt with so far have been filtered through an individual mind, and whereas, like any other piece of literature, they grew out of a certain age and tradition of thought, it is dangerous to overrate their importance either as mirrors of the existing order or as projectors of a new order. While again and again the dream of a utopian in one age has become the reality of the next, as O'Shaughnessy sings in his famous verses, the exact connection between the two can only be guessed at, and rarely, I suppose, can it be traced. It would be a little foolish to attempt to prove that the inventor of the modern incubator was a student of Sir Thomas More.

Up to the present the idola which have exercised the most considerable influence upon the actual life of the community are such as have been partly expressed in a hundred works and never perhaps fully expressed in one. In order to distinguish these idola from those that have occupied us till now, we should perhaps call them collective utopias or social myths. There is a considerable literature that relates to these myths

[193]

in French, one of the best known works being M. George Sorel's Reflections on Violence; and in practice it is sometimes rather hard to tell where the Utopia leaves off and the social myth begins.

The history of mankind's social myths has still in the main to be written. There is a partial attempt at this over a limited period in Mr. Henry Osborn Taylor's The Mediæval Mind; but this is only a beginning, and other ages are almost untouched. The type of myth that concerns us here is not the pure action myth which M. Sorel has analyzed; we are rather interested in those myths which are, as it were, the ideal content of the existing order of things, myths which, by being consciously formulated and worked out in thought, tend to perpetuate and perfect that order. This type of social myth approaches very closely to the classic utopia, and we could divide it, similarly, into myths of escape and myths of reconstruction. Thus the myth of political freedom, for example, as formulated by the writers of the American revolution, frequently serves as an excellent refuge for disturbed consciences when the Department of Justice or the Immigration Bureau has been a little too assiduous in its harassment of political agitators.

Unfortunately, it has become a habit to look upon our idola as particularly fine and exalted, and as representing the better side of human nature. As a matter of fact, the myths which are created in a community under religious, political, or economic influences cannot be characterized as either good or bad: their nature is defined by their capacity to help men to react creatively upon their environment and to develop a humane life. We have still to recognize that a belief in these idola

[194]

is not by itself a creditable attitude. Even quite base and stupid people are frequently governed by ideals; indeed, it is the ideals that are in many cases responsible for their baseness and stupidity. Neither is the habit of responding to idola any evidence of rational thought. People respond to "ideas"—that is, to word-patterns—as they respond to the stimulus of light or heat, because they are human beings and not because they are philosophers, and they respond to projections, to idola, for the same reason, and not because they are saints. Our myths may be the outcome of rational thought and practice or not; but the response to these myths is not perhaps more than ten times in a hundred the result of following the processes of reason from beginning to end.

We must think of our idola as a sort of diffused environment or atmosphere, which differs in "chemical content" and in extension with each individual. Some of these idola have so uniformly taken possession of men's minds in a particular age that they are as much a part of the environment a baby is born into as the furniture of his house. The sociologists who follow Emile Durkheim have called a certain part of these idola collective representations but they are wrong, I believe, when they limit these "representations" to savage or ignorant groups for they are an important part of every civilized person's luggage. Parallel with The Story of Mankind and with The Story of Utopias, which I have just told, it would be amusing to write The Story of Mankind's Myths. This work, however, would require the scholarship and industry of another Leibniz, and all that I wish to do here is to put together the chief social myths that have played a part in Western Europe and America during the modern period, to contrast these idola with the utopias of the past and the partial remedies for the present, and to suggest the bearing of all this upon any new departures we may be ready to make.

In selecting these idola—The Country House, Coketown, the Megalopolis—I have been forced to gauge their strength and test their quality very largely by their actual results in the workaday world, and it is a little hard to purify them from the various institutions, old and new, in which they are mixt. Yet with all this taint of actuality, these idola are scarcely as credible as the Republic and it will help matters a little to realize that we are still within the province of utopia, and may exercise all the utopian privileges.

2

To understand the utopia of the Country House we must jump back a few centuries in history.

Anyone who has ranged through the European castles that were built before the fourteenth century will realize that they were no more built for comfort than is a modern battleship. They were essentially garrisons of armed men whose main occupation was theft, violence, and murder; and every feature of their environment reflected the necessities of their life. These castles would be found beetling a cliff or a steep hill; their walls and their buttresses would be made of huge, rough hewn stones; their living arrangements would resemble those of a barracks with an almost complete lack of what we now regard as the normal decencies and privacies, except possibly for the lord and his lady;

[196]

and the life of these feudal bands was necessarily a crude and limited one.

Up to the fourteenth century in Western Europe the little fortified town, or the unfortified town that lay beneath the protection of a garrison on a hill, was the only other social unit that competed with the even more limited horizons of the peasant's village, or with the spacious claims for the Here and the Hereafter which were put forward by the Roman Church. To dream of huge metropolises and farflung armies and food brought from the ends of the earth would have been wilder in those days than anything More pictured in his Utopia.

During the fifteenth century in England, and in other parts of Europe the same thing seems to have happened sooner or later, this life of agriculture and warfare and petty trade was upset: the feudal power of the reigning nobles was concentrated in the hands of a supreme lord, the King; and the King and his archives and his court settled in the National Capital, instead of moving about from place to place in the troubled realm. The territories of the feudal lords ceased to be dispersed; their possessions were confined more and more within what were called national boundaries; and instead of remaining in their castles the great lords gave up their crude, barbaric ways, and went up to the capital to be civilized. In the course of time money took the place of direct tribute; instead of receiving wheat and eggs and labor, the lord came into possession of a rent which could be figured in pence and pounds; a rent which could be transferred to the new trading cities for the goods which the rest of the world had for sale. There is a fascinating picture of this change

[197]

in W. J. Ashley's Economic History; and the old life itself is outlined, with a wealth of significant detail, in J. S. Fletcher's Memorials of a Yorkshire Parish.

At the same time that this change was taking place in the physical life of Western Europe, a corresponding change was taking place in the domain of culture. Digging about the ruins of Rome and other cities, the men of the late Middle Age discovered the remains of a great and opulent civilization; and exploring the manuscripts and printed books which were getting into general circulation, they found themselves face to face with strange conceptions of life, with habits of refinement, ease, and sensuous luxury which the hard life of the camp and the castle had never really permitted. There followed a reaction against their old life which was little less than a revulsion; and in that reaction two great institutions fell out of fashion. Men ceased to build castles to protect themselves against physical dangers; and they left off entering monasteries in order to fortify their souls for the Hereafter. Both the spiritual and the temporal life began to shift to a new institution, the Country House. The idolum of the Country House drew together and coalesced; and as a familiar symbol of this change the colleges at Oxford which date from the Renascence can scarcely be distinguished in architectural detail from the palaces which the aristocracy were building in the same period; while our banks and our political edifices to this day bear almost universally the stamp of that Roman and Grecian litter which men discovered on the outskirts of the mediæval city.

3

We do not know the Country House until we realize, to begin with, what its physical characteristics are like. There are a great many descriptions which the reader may consult if he does not happen to live in the neighborhood of a great Country House: but perhaps instead of examining the contemporary Country House it will be well to go back to its beginnings, and see how it was pictured in all its encrusted splendor at the first movement of the Renascence—in the setting which François Rabelais, in one of the few downright serious passages in his great work, Gargantua, sought to provide for the good life.

Gargantua purposes to build a new Abbey which he calls the Abbey of Theleme. This Abbey is to be in every respect what the mediæval Abbey was not. Hence to begin with, the Abbey, unlike the castle, is to lie in the midst of the open country; and unlike the monastery, it is to have no walls. Every member is to be furnished with a generous apartment, consisting of a principal room, a withdrawing room, a handsome closet, a wardrobe, and an oratory; and the house itself is to contain not merely libraries in every language, but fair and spacious galleries of paintings. Besides these lodgings there is to be a tilt-yard, a riding court, a theatre, or public playhouse, and a natatory or place to swim. By the river, for the Abbey is to be situated on the Loire, there is to be a Garden of Pleasure, and between two of the six towers of the hexagon, in which form the building is arranged, there are courts for tennis and other games. Add to this orchards full of fruit trees, parks abounding with venison, and an archery range, fill all the halls and chambers with rich tapestries, cover all the pavements and floors with green cloth—and the furnishing of the Abbey of Theleme is complete.

The costumes of the inmates are equally splendid and elaborate. In order to have the accoutrements of the ladies' and gentlemen's toilets more convenient, there was to be "about the wood of Theleme a row of houses to the extent of half a league, very neat and cleanly, wherein dwelt the goldsmiths, lapidaries, jewellers, embroiderers, tailors, gold drawers, velvet weavers, tapestry makers, and upholsterers. . . ." They were to be "furnished with matter and stuff from the hands of Lord Nausiclete, who every year brought them seven ships from the Perlas and Cannibal Islands, laden with ingots of gold, with raw silk, with pearls and precious stones."

The women who are admitted to Theleme must be fair, well-featured, and of sweet disposition; the men must be comely and well-conditioned. Everyone is to be admitted freely and allowed to depart freely; and instead of attempting to practice poverty, chastity, and obedience, the inmates may be honorably married, may be rich, and may live at liberty.

The liberty of Theleme is indeed complete; it is such a liberty as one enjoys at a Country House to this day, under the care of a tactful hostess; for everyone does nothing except follow his own free will and pleasure, rising out of his bed whenever he thinks good, and eating, drinking, and laboring when he has a mind to it. In all their rule and strictest tie of their order, as Rabelais puts it, there is but one clause to be observed—

"Do what you please."

[200]

4

When we turn our attention from Rabelais' conceit of an anti-monastic order, we discover that he has given us an excellent picture of the Country House, and of what I shall take the liberty of calling Country House culture. We see pretty much the same outlines in the introduction to Boccaccio's Decameron; it is elaborately described in terms of that most complete of Country Houses, Hampton Court, in Pope's Rape of the Lock; it is vividly pictured by Meredith in his portrait of The Egoist; and it is analyzed in Mr. H. G. Wells' cruel description of Bladesover in Tono-Bungay, as well as by Mr. Bernard Shaw in Heartbreak House. Whether Mr. W. H. Mallock holds the pattern of Country House culture up to us in The New Republic or Anton Chekhov penetrates its aimlessness and futility in The Cherry Orchard, The Country House is one of the recurrent themes of literature.

This renascence idolum of the Country House, then, is powerful and complete: I know no other pattern which has imposed its standards and its practices with such complete success upon the greater part of European civilization. While the Country House was in the beginning an aristocratic institution, it has penetrated now to every stratum of society; and although we may not immediately see the connection, it is responsible, I believe, for the particular go and direction which the industrial revolution has taken. The Country House standards of consumption are responsible for our Acquisitive Society.

5

Perhaps the shortest way to suggest the character

of Country House institutions is to say that they are the precise opposite of everything that Plato looked upon as desirable in a good community.

The Country House is concerned not with the happiness of the whole community but with the felicity of the governors. The conditions which underly this limited and partial good life are political power and economic wealth; and in order for the life to flourish, both of these must be obtained in almost limitless quantities. The chief principles that characterize this society are possession and passive enjoyment.

Now, in the Country House possession is based upon privilege and not upon work. The title to land which was historically obtained for the most part through force and fraud is the economic foundation of the Country House existence. In order to keep the artisans and laborers who surround the Country House at their work, it is necessary to keep them from having access to the land on their own account, provision always being made that the usufruct of the land shall go to the owner and not to the worker. This emphasis upon passive ownership points to the fact that in the Country House there is no active communion between the people and their environment. Such activities as remain in the Country House—the pursuit of game, for instance—rest upon imitating in play activities which once had a vital use or prepared for some vital function, as a child's playing with a doll is a preparation for motherhood. The Country House ideal is that of a completely functionless existence; or at best, an existence in which all the functions that properly belong to a civilized man shall be carried on by functionaries. Since this ideal cannot be realized in the actual world,

[202]

for the reason that it is completely at odds with man's biological inheritance, it is necessary in the Country House utopia to fill in by play and sport an otherwise desirable vacuity.

In the Country House literature and the fine arts undoubtedly flourish: but they flourish as the objects of appreciation rather than as the active, creative elements in the community's life; they flourish particularly in the fashion that Plato looked upon as a corrupting influence in the community. In the arts, a gourmandizing habit of mind—the habit of receiving things and being played upon by them—prevails; so that instead of the ability to share creative ecstasy, the chief canon of judgment is "taste," a certain capacity to discriminate among sensory stimuli, a capacity which is essentially just as hospitable to a decomposing cheese as to the very staff of life. The effect of this gourmandism in the arts can be detected in every element of the Country House from cellar to roof; for the result has been to emphasize the collection of good things rather than their creation, and there is an aspect in which the Country House is little better than a robber's hoard or a hunter's cache—a miniature anticipation of the modern museums of natural history and art.

Observe the architecture of our Country House. If it has been built in England during the last three hundred years, the style is probably that bastard Greek or Roman which we call Renascence architecture; if the Country House was built in America during the last thirty years, it is as likely as not a Tudor residence with traces of castle fortification left here and there on the façade. On the walls there will be plenty of

[203]

paintings; indeed a whole gallery may be devoted to them. In all probability, however, the paintings have been created in other times by men long since dead, and in other countries: there may be a portrait by Rembrandt, a Persian miniature, a print by Hokusai. Some very fine element in the structure, a fireplace or a bit of panelling, may have been removed piece by piece from the original Country House in England, Italy, or France; even as many features of the original Country House were quarried, perhaps, from some mediæval abbey. The very china that we use upon our tables nowadays is a Country House importation which took the place of pewter and earthenware; and wall paper is another importation. From feature to feature everything is derivative; everything, in the last analysis, has either been stolen or purchased from the original makers; and what has not been stolen or purchased has been basely copied.

The insatiability of the Country House to possess art is only equalled by its inability to create it. In the Country House, the arts are not married to the community, but are kept for its pleasure.

Let there be no confusion as to either the facts or the ideal we are examining. There is a vast difference between that fine mingling of traditions which is the very breath of the arts, as the lover of classic Greek statuary knows, and the rapacious imperialistic habit of looting the physical objects of art which has been the essence of the Country House method in modern times, even as it seems to have been a couple of thousand years ago in the Roman villa. A genuine culture will borrow steadily from other cultures; but it will go to them as the bee goes to the flower for pollen, and

[204]

not as the beekeeper goes to the hive for honey. There is a creative borrowing and a possessive borrowing; and the Country House has in the main limited itself to possessive borrowing. The Country House ideal, in fact, is limitless possession: so the great Country House masters have five or six houses, perhaps, in their name, although they need but a single one to cover their heads.

Now the Country House idolum involves a dissociation between the Country House and the community in which it is placed. If you will take the trouble to examine mediæval conditions, you will find that differences of rank and wealth did not make a very great difference between the life of the lord in his castle, and his retainers: if the common man could not claim to be as good as his lord, it is plain that the lord shared most of the common man's disabilities, and was, for all the exaggerations of chivalry, just as ignorant, just as illiterate, just as coarse. In the cities, too, the lowest workman in the guild shared the institutions of his masters: the churches, the guild pageants, and the morality plays were all part and parcel of the same culture.

The Country House changed this condition. Culture came to mean not a participation in the creative activities of one's own community, but the acquisition of the products of other communities; and it scarcely matters much whether these acquisitions were within the spiritual or the material domain. There had of course been the beginnings of such a split in mediæval literature, with its vulgar Rabelaisian tales and its refined romances of the court; but with the integration of the Country House idolum, this divorcement was accentuated in every other activity of the community. One of the results of this split was that popular institutions were deprived of their contacts with the general world of culture, and languished away; or they were transformed, as the public schools of England were transformed into restricted upper class institutions. Far more important than this, perhaps, was the fact that each separate Country House was forced to obtain for its limited circle all the elements that were necessary to the good life in a whole community such as Plato described. We shall deal with the effects of this presently.

6

Let us admit what is valid in the utopia of the Country House. Enjoyment is a necessary element in achievement, and by its regard for the decent graces of life, for such things as an ease in manners and a fine flow of conversation and the clash of wits and a sensitiveness to beautiful things, the Country House was by all odds a humanizing influence. In so far as the Country House fostered a belief in contemplation and a desire for the arts apart from any uses that might be made of them by way of civic advertisement; in so far as it urged that all our pragmatic activities must be realized in things that are worth having or doing for themselves, the Country House was right, eminently right. It was no snobbery on the part of Russian soviet officialism when it opened up some of its Country Houses as rest houses for the peasants and workers, and then insisted that some of the airs of the Country House should be acquired there, to replace the rough usages of the stable, the dungpile, and the field. Ruskin and Samuel Butler were possibly right when they insisted that the perfect gentleman was a finer product than the perfect peasant or artisan: he is a finer product because he is essentially more alive. Even by its emphasis upon appreciation the Country House did no mean service; for it called attention to the fact that there were more permanent standards— standards which were common to the arts of Greece and China—than those which were looked upon as sufficient in the local region. In sum, the Country House emphasized a human best, which was the sum of a dozen partial perfections; and so all that was crude and inadequate in the old regional cultures was brought to light and criticized. All these virtues I admit; and they hold just as good today as they ever did.

The fatal weakness of Country House culture comes out all the plainer for this admission. The Country House did not see that enjoyment rested upon achievement, and was indeed inseparable from achievement. The Country House strove to put achievement in one compartment and enjoyment in another; with the result that the craftsman who no longer had the capacity to enjoy the fine arts no longer had the ability to create them. The effect of an isolated routine of enjoyment is equally debilitating; for enjoyment, to the masters of the Country House came too easily, with a mere snap of the fingers, as it were, and the tendency of connoisseurship was to set novelty above intrinsic worth. Hence the succession of styles by which Country House decoration has become a thing for mockery: Chinese in one age, Indian in another, Persian in the next, with Egyptian, Middle African, and heaven knows what else destined to follow in due order. There is nothing to settle to, because there is no task to be done, and no problem to work out; and as soon as the first taste for a style gets exhausted it is speedily supplanted by another.

It would be impossible to calculate the extent to which the Country House has degraded our taste, but I have little doubts as to the source of the degradation. The stylicism which has perverted the arts and has kept a congruent modern style from developing has been the work of Country House culture. I remember well the contempt with which a furniture manufacturer in the Chiltern Hills told me about the way in which he produced an original Sheraton: his knowledge of sound furniture design was subordinated to some other person's knowledge of "style" and the miscarriage of the man's innate craftsmanship made him so mordant on the subject that it seemed as though he had been reading Thorstein Veblen's Theory of the Leisure Class. It is the same through all the arts. A visit to the industrial sections of the Metropolitan Museum in New York will show how dismally the taste for novelty, which led the Sheratons and Chippendales to find "classic motifs" in one age, causes the designers of the present day to seek the motifs of Sheraton and Chippendale. So much for what happened to the arts when enjoyment and achievement are separated.

7

The industrial bearing of the Renascence ideal is of capital importance.

During the Middle Age the emphasis in industry was upon the production of tangible goods; the craft guilds

[208]

set high standards in design and workmanship; and the aim of the worker, in most of the trades, was to get a living from his work, and not simply to get enough money to free himself from the necessity of working. This is a broad generalization, I need scarcely emphasize, and there is plenty of evidence of pecuniary interests under the best of conditions; but it seems fair to say that the dominant ideals of the older industrial order were industrial rather than commercial. In the trading ventures that the Country House promoted under its Drakes and Raleighs, ventures which were needed to bring them "Ships from the Perlas and Cannibal Islands," the emphasis shifted from workmanship to sale; and the notion of working and gambling to acquire multifarious goods took the place of that earlier ideal which Henry Adams so sympathetically described in Mt. St. Michel and Chartres. Thus the good life, as I have said elsewhere, was the Goods Life: it could be purchased. If the whole community no longer offered the conditions for this life, one might filch what one wanted from the general store, and try to monopolize for self or family all that was needed for a good life in the community.

What is the chief economic outcome of this ideal? The chief outcome, I think, is to exaggerate the demand for goods, and to cause an enormously wasteful duplication of the apparatus of consumption. If the limit to one's possessions should be simply the extent of one's purse; if happiness is to be acquired through obtaining the comforts and luxuries of life; if a man who possesses a single house is considered fortunate, and a man who possesses five houses five times as fortunate; if there are no standards of living other than the in-

[209]

satiable one that has been set up in the Country House
—well, then there is really no limit to the business of
getting and spending, and our lives become the mean
handiwork of coachman, cook, and groom. Our Country
House will not merely be a house: there will be a chapel,
an art gallery, a theater, a gymnasium, as François
Rabelais imagined. As the common possessions of the
community dwindle, the private possessions of individuals are multiplied; and at last, there remains no other
community than a multitude of anarchic individuals,
each of whom is doing his best to create for himself a
Country House, notwithstanding the fact that the net
result of his endeavors—this is the drab tragedy and
the final thing to be said against it—is perhaps nothing
better than six inadequate rooms at the end of nowhere
in a Philadelphia suburb.

The Country House, then, is the chief pattern by
means of which the mediæval order was transformed
into the modern order. It does not matter very much
whether the Country House is an estate on Long Island
or a cottage in Montclair; whether it is a house in
Golder's Green or a family manor in Devonshire: these
are essentially affairs of scale, and the underlying identity is plain enough. The idolum of the Country House
prevails even when quarters are taken up in the midst
of the metropolis. More than ever the Country House
today tries to make up by an abundance of physical
goods for all that has been lost through its divorce
from the underlying community; more than ever it
attempts to be self-sufficient within the limits of suburbia. The automobile, the phonograph, and the radio-
telephone have only served to increase this self-suffi-
ciency; and I need not show at length how these instru-

mentalities have deepened the elements of acquisitiveness and passive, uncreative, mechanical enjoyment.

The Country House's passionate demand for physical goods has given rise to another institution, Coketown; and it is the idolum of Coketown, the industrial age's contribution to the Country House, that we have now to consider.

8

The chief difference between the individual utopias of the nineteenth century and the "collective representation" of Coketown is that these individual utopias were concerned to repair certain points where Manchester, Newark, Pittsburgh, and Elberfeld-Barmen fell short of the ideal. In repairing these points, Bellamy and Hertzka were ready to alter the conventional arrangements by which property and land were held, and capital was accumulated. The final end however was the same; and the differences are therefore more apparent than real.

If the illustrative example of the Country House is in the Abbey of Theleme, that of Coketown is in the sharp picture of industrialism which Charles Dickens presents in Hard Times.

Coketown, as Dickens sees it, is the quintessence of the industrial age. It is perhaps one of the few idola of the modern world which has no parallel in any earlier civilization that we have been able to explore. In order to understand what Coketown brought into the world, we must realize that before Coketown came into existence the center of every important European city consisted of a marketplace, shadowed over by a Cathedral, a Market Court, and a Guildhall; and frequently there

[211]

would be an adjacent university. This was the typical formation. The various quarters of the city were subordinated to these central institutions, and the work which was carried on within the city's walls was more or less concretely realized in the local community.

Coketown, on the other hand, was the outcome of other conditions and necessities. The center of Coketown's activity was the mill, set at first in the open country near falling water, and then as coal was applied to steam engines, removed to areas more accessible to the coal fields. The factory became the new social unity; in fact it became the only social unit; and, as Dickens sharply put it, "the jail looked like the town hall, and the town hall like the infirmary"— and all of them looked like the factory, a gaunt building of murky brick that once was red or yellow. The sole object of the factory is to produce goods for sale; and every other institution is encouraged in Coketown only to the extent that it does not seriously interfere with this aim.

What are the outward physical aspects of Coketown? To begin with, the city is laid out by an engineer; it is laid out with a mathematical correctness and with a complete disregard for the amenities. If there are hills where Coketown ought to stand, the hills are leveled; if there are swamps, the swamps are filled; if there are lakes, the lakes are drained away. The pattern to which Coketown's activities are fitted is that of the gridiron; there are no deviations and no allowances in the working out of this plan; never will a street swerve as much as a hair's breadth to save a stand of trees or open up a vista. In the matter of transportation and intercourse, the aim of Coketown is to "get somewhere"; and it fancies that by laying down straight lines and joining them in rectangles this aim is expedited; despite the demonstration in every city of older growth that a radial system of intercommunication is much more economical than the gridiron. As a result, there is no terminus to any of the avenues of Coketown; for they begin on a draughting board and end in infinity. It is impossible to approach from the front the jails, hospitals, and sanatoria of which Coketown boasts; the tendency is to run past them. So much for the physical layout of the industrial city; what remains is obscured by smoke.

The factory is the center of Coketown's social life; and it is here that the greater part of the population spend their days. At its purest, that is to say, during the first half of the nineteenth century, and in a great many centers to this day, the factory is the only institution that provides anything like a social life, in spite of the fact that the unremitting toil which accompanies its routine reduces the graces of social intercourse to such a minimum that drunkenness and copulation are the only amusements which the inhabitants can engage in as a relief from their noble duty of providing the rest of the world with necessities, comforts, luxuries, and nullities.

The Coketown idolum has been disintegrating a little during the last two decades, under the influence of the garden cities movement, and I am aware that in certain departments I am celebrating a lost cause and an abandoned idealism; but there still remain in acres and acres of workingmen's dwellings, such as one finds in Battersea and Philadelphia, and in old-fashioned railway stations, and in buildings like the Mechanics Halls of

Pittsburgh and Boston, a notion of what Coketown stood for when Coketown, the Frankenstein which had been created by the Country House, had not been repudiated by its master.

Coketown is devoted to the production of material goods; and there is no good in Coketown that does not derive from this aim. The only enjoyment which those who are inured to the Coketown routine can participate in is mechanical achievement; that is to say, activity along industrial and commercial lines; and the only result of this achievement is—more achievement. It follows that all the standards of Coketown are of a quantitative kind; so many score of machines, so many tons of gew-gaws, so many miles of piping, so many dollars of profit. The opportunities for self-assertion and constructiveness in such a community are practically boundless; and I can never confront the mechanical felicities of a printing plant without realizing how fascinating these opportunities are, and how deeply they satisfy certain elements in our nature. The unfortunate thing about Coketown, however, is that these are the only sort of opportunities that are available; and work whose standards are of a qualitative sort, the work of scholars and artists and scientists, is either frozen out of the community by deliberate ostracism, or is hitched to the machine; the artist, for example, being compelled to sing the praises of Coketown's goods or to paint the portrait of Coketown's supreme esthetic achievement—the Self-Made Man.

In its pristine state, Coketown is not a complete community. So it is natural that the idolum should have provided certain additions. In the first place, the activities of Coketown, whether they are beneficial or

[214]

wasteful, satisfy only certain elements in the human makeup; and although much may be done by compulsory education to discipline the younger generation to the machine, and to show them the necessity of doing nothing which would interfere with the continued activity of the machine—for work in Coketown, as Samuel Butler fearfully predicted in Erewhon, is in the main simply attendance upon machinery—here and there the igneous instincts of the workers will break through the solidified layer of habit which the school and the factory have produced, and the arcane energies of the population will flow either into the Country House or into that other simulacrum of the civic life, Broadway.

Coketown for the workaday week, the Country House for the weekend, is the compromise that has been practically countenanced; although the country houses of the working classes may be nothing more than a diminutive extension of the urban slum near sea or mountain. But it must be admitted that there is a permanent Country House and a permanent Coketown population in the more ideal aspects of the order. Mr. Wells in the Time Machine has given a picture of Coketown which is perhaps a little exuberant in some of its details— the picture of a happy and careless Country House population, living on the surface of the earth, mid all the graces of a jolly weekend, and that of the factory population, the Morlocks, living in the bowels of the earth and performing the necessary industrial functions. Mr. Wells' presentation is a little exaggerated, however, and we must be content here with such a plain and outright description as Messrs. Bounderby and Gradgrind would approve of.

In the Coketown scheme of things, all that does not contribute to the physical necessities of life is called a comfort; and all that does not contribute either to comforts or necessities is called a luxury. These three grades of good correspond to the three classes of the population: the necessities are for the lower order of manual workers, together with such accessory members as clerks, teachers, and minor officials; the comforts are for the comfortable classes, that is, the small order of merchants, bankers, and industrialists; while the luxuries are for the aristocracy, if there is such an hereditary group, and for such as are able to lift themselves out of the two previous orders. Chief among the luxuries, it goes without saying, are art and literature and any of the other permanent interests of a humane life.

Let us note what an improvement the three classes of Coketown are upon the three classes in Plato's Republic. The custom of limiting the earnings of the working classes to the margin of subsistence is singularly effective in keeping them occupied with the business of production—as long as there is no overplus in the market to throw them out of work—and it is thus a safeguard of efficiency and industry which Plato, who was deplorably obtuse in these matters, did not provide. It is likewise obvious that the life of a middle class citizen, with plenty to eat and drink, with his life protected by the policeman, his pocketbook protected by the insurance company, his spiritual happiness protected by the church, his human sympathies protected by the charity organization society, his intelligence protected by the newspaper, and his economic privileges protected by the State—this middle class citizen is, after all, a much more fortunate and happy individual than those Platonic warriors whose life was a perpetual effort to keep the edge on their bodies and minds. As for the Guardians of the State, it is plain that Plato did not offer them any inducement to do their work which would attract a normal commercial man: anyone who was worth a hundred thousand dollars a year would have thought twice before assuming leadership in Plato's impoverished commonwealth, whereas in Coketown he would find that his simple ability to make money would be taken as sufficient proof of his education, his insight, and his wisdom in every department of life. More than that, Coketown, when all is said and done, welcomes the artist with a cordiality that puts Plato to shame: Coketown can afford its luxuries since, when you look at the matter squarely, a rare painting might be worth as much as a rare postage stamp; and it is accordingly an acceptable addition to the Coketown milieu.

Coketown has, in fact, only one question for the arts to answer: What are they good for? If the answer can be expressed in money, the art in question is taken to be almost as satisfactory as a device to save labor, to increase speed, or to multiply the output.

9

There is one phenomenon still to be accounted for in the economy of Coketown; one monumental instrument without which the wheels of Coketown would become clogged and the very breath of Coketown be extinguished.

I refer to the rubbish heaps.

The aim of production in Coketown is naturally more

production, and it is only by making things sufficiently shoddy to go to pieces quickly, or by changing the fashion sufficiently often, that the machinery of Coke-town can for the most part be kept running. The rage and fury of Coketown's production has to be balanced off by an equal rage and fury of consumption—continence would be fatal. As a result, nothing in Coketown is finished or permanent or settled: these qualities are another name for death. Coketown makes china to be broken, clothes to be worn out, and houses to be torn down; and if something remains over from an earlier age which made things more soundly, it is either incarcerated in a museum, and derided as the monument of a non-progressive age, or it is demolished as a nuisance. So powerful is the idolum of Coketown that in the workaday world building after building continues to meet with irreparable ruin at the hands of barbarians from Coketown: why, I have even seen innocent little half-timbered fifteenth century cottages whose fronts were obliterated by a nineteenth century plasterer, in the name of progress.

The status of every family in Coketown can be told by the size of its rubbish heap. In fact, to "make a pile" in the markets of Coketown is ultimately to make another pile—of dust and junk and litter—on the edge of the town where the factory district dribbles off into the open country. So in Coketown consumption is not merely a necessity: it is a social duty, a means of keeping "the wheels of civilization turning." At times there appears to be a possibility that this utopia may defeat its purposes by producing goods at such a pace that the rubbish heaps will fall behind the demands of the market; and while this mars the theoretic perfection

[218]

of the Coketown social organization, it is offset by periods of war, when the market is practically inexhaustible, and Coketown's prosperity increases to a point at which the working classes are on the point of becoming the comfortable classes without having had sufficient previous training to make their contribution to the rubbish heap—a serious pass, amidst which confusion the working classes of Coketown might take to reducing their working days and enjoying their leisure without sufficient consumptive effort.

This, then, is the idolum of Coketown. There are certain features in it which need to be noticed. The first is that there is a certain solid reality in Coketown that remains when all its pretensions and idiocies have been incinerated. An environment that is devoted solely to the production of material goods is obviously no sort of environment for a good community, for life is more than a matter of finding what we shall eat and wherewithal we shall be clothed: it is an interaction with a whole world of landscapes, living creatures and ideas, in comparison with which Coketown is a mere blister on the earth's surface. Nevertheless, with respect to the business of melting steel and building roads and performing certain essential industrial operations, the aims of Coketown are, up to a certain point, relevant: we have already encountered them in Andreæ's Christianopolis. There is no need to dismiss the good that lies inside of industrialism because it does not embrace the good that lies beyond it.

Up to a certain point, then, using mechanical power rather than human power is good; so is large-scale production, so is the division of labor and division of operation; so is rapid transportation; so is the accurate

[219]

methodology of the engineer; and so are various other features in the modern industrial world. One might even say a word for efficiency, as against "doing things rather more or less." Coketown made the horrid mistake of believing that all these things were good in themselves. New factories, for example, drew a bigger population into the city: Coketown did not perceive that, as Plato pointed out, beyond a certain point the city as a social unit would cease to exist. Bigger and better was Coketown's motto; and it resolutely refused to see that there was no necessary connection between these adjectives. The whole case for and against Coketown rests upon our admission of the phrase "up to a certain point." Up to a certain point, industrialism is good, especially in its modern, neotechnic, electrical phase: Coketown, on the other hand, believes that there is no limit to the usefulness of industrialism.

Up to a certain point—but what point? The answer is, up to the point at which the cultivation of a humane life in a community of humane people becomes difficult or impossible.

Men come together, says Aristotle, to live; they remain together in order to live the good life. This determination of the good life is the only check and balance that we can have upon Coketown; and it is perhaps because we have been so little concerned with it that the practical effect of the Coketown idolum has been so devastating. "Invention and organization," as Mr. George Santayana admirably points out, "which ought to have increased leisure by producing the necessaries of life with little labor, have only increased the population, degraded labor, and diffused luxury." William Morris conceived that men in the future might

[220]

discard many complicated machines because they could live more happily, aye, work more happily without them. Whether indeed a good part of modern organization and machinery could be scrapt is perhaps a debatable question: but the possibility of scrapping it is at least conceivable once we become more interested in the actual result of industrialism upon the life and happiness of the people who are part of the organization than we are in the profits which pile up upon paper, and are finally realized in an ever-growing rubbish heap.

10

By what means can the Country House keep Coketown working for it? The idolum of the Country House, which was built up during the Renascence, and the idolum of Coketown, which was formed in the early part of the nineteenth century, are obviously two separate worlds; and in order that each might be realized in our daily life, it was necessary that some connecting tissue be manufactured to keep them together. This tissue was the social myth, the collective utopia, of the National State.

There is a sense in which we may look upon the National State as a fact; but that great philosopher of the National State, Mazzini, realized that the National State had continually to be willed; and its existence lies plainly, therefore, on a different plane from the existence of a bit of territory, a building, or a city. In fact, it is only by the persistent projection of this utopia for the last three or four hundred years that its existence has become credible; for all the minute descriptions which the political historian gives to the

National State, its origins and its institutions and its
people, read a good deal like that fine story which Hans
Andersen told about the king who walked the streets
naked because two rascally tailors had persuaded him
that they had woven and cut up for him a beautiful
outfit of clothes.

It will help us to appreciate this beautiful fabrication
of the National State if we turn aside for a moment and
glance at the actual world as it is known to the geographer and the anthropologist. Here are the physical
facts in defiance of which the utopia of nationalism has
been clapped together.

11

The earth that the geographer surveys is divided into
five great land masses. These land masses in turn can
be broken up into a number of natural regions, each of
which has within its rough and approximate frontiers
a certain complex of soil, climate, vegetation, and, arising out of these, certain primitive occupations which
the inhabitants of the region originally practiced and
later, through the advance of trade and invention,
elaborated. Between these natural regions there are
occasionally frontiers, such as the barrier of the Pyre-
nees which separates "France" from "Spain"; but these
barriers have never altogether prevented movements of
population from one area to another. In order to have
a more faithful knowledge of regional groupings in
certain important areas, the reader might with profit
consult Professor Fleure's Human Geography in Western Europe. (London: Williams and Norgate.)

These natural regions are the groundwork of human
regions; that is, the non-political grouping of popula-

tion with respect to soil, climate, vegetation, animal life, industry and historic tradition. In each of these human regions we find that the population does not consist of a multitude of atomic individuals: on the contrary, when the geographer plots houses and buildings on a topographic map, he finds that people and houses cohere together in groups of more or less limited size, called cities, towns, villages, hamlets. Normally, a vast amount of intercourse takes place between these groupings; and in the Middle Age, before the utopia of the National State had been created, the pilgrim and the wandering scholar and the journeyman and the strolling player could have been met with on all the highways of Europe. Under the dispensation of the National State, however, the population, as the German economist Buecher points out, tends to be more settled, and we transport goods rather than people. It is important to realize that, so far as the geographer can discover, this trade and intercourse between local groups has been a part of Western European civilization since Neolithic times, at least: it takes place continually between individuals and corporate groups in one place and another, and as far as geographical facts are concerned might more easily exist between Dover and Calais, let us say, than between Calais and Paris.

Now the interesting thing about the utopia of the National State is that it has only the most casual relation to the facts of geography. Wherever it suits the purposes of the Guardians of the State, the facts are ignored, and an artificial relation is *willed* into existence. The human communities which the regional sociologist recognizes do not always coincide with those which the statesman wishes to incorporate as "national

[223]

territory," and when this conflict occurs, the idea rather than the reality triumphs, if necessary by brute force.

In the utopia of the National State there are no natural regions; and the equally natural grouping of people in towns, villages and cities, which, as Aristotle points out, is perhaps the chief distinction between man and the other animals, is tolerated only upon the fiction that the State hands over to these groups a portion of its omnipotent authority, or "sovereignty" as it is called, and permits them to exercise a corporate life. Unfortunately for this beautiful myth, which generations of lawyers and statesmen have labored to build up, cities existed long before states—there was a Rome on the Tiber long before there was a Roman Imperium—and the gracious permission of the state is simply a perfunctory seal upon the accomplished fact.

Instead of recognizing natural regions and natural groups of people, the utopia of nationalism establishes, by the surveyor's line, a certain realm called national territory, and makes all the inhabitants of this territory the members of a single, indivisible group, the nation, which is supposed to be prior in claim and superior in power to all other groups. This is the only social formation that is officially recognized within the national utopia. What is common to all the inhabitants of this territory is thought to be of far greater importance than any of the things that bind men together in particular civic or industrial groups.

Let us look at this world of national utopias. The contrast between the politician's map and the geographer's would be little less than amazing were our eyes not used to it, and were we not taught in modern times to look upon it as inevitable. Instead of the natural grouping of land masses and regions, one finds a multitude of quite arbitrary lines: boundaries like those that separate Canada and the United States or Belgium and the Netherlands are just as frequent as the natural frontier of sea that surrounds England. Sometimes these national territories are big, and sometimes they are little; but the bigness of empires like those of France, England, or the United States is not due to any essential identity of interests between the sundry communities of these empires, but to the fact that they are forcibly held together by a political government. National lines, in other words, continue to exist only as long as the inhabitants continue to act in terms of them; are ready to pay their taxes to support customs bureaux, immigration offices, frontier patrols, and educational systems; and are prepared, in the last extremity, to lay down their lives to prevent other groups from crossing these imaginary lines without permission.

The chief concern of the national utopia is the support of the central government, for the government is the guardian of territory and privilege. The principal business of that government is to keep the territory properly defined, and to increase its limits, when possible, so as to make the taxable area larger. By stressing the importance of these concerns, and constantly playing up the dangers of rivalry from other national utopias, the State builds a bridge between the Country House and Coketown, and persuades the workers in Coketown that they have more in common with the classes that exploit them than they have in common with other groups within a more limited community. It would seem that this reconciliation of Coketown and the Country House is little less than miraculous, even as an ideal; and perhaps it would be interesting to examine a little more carefully the apparatus by which this is effected.

12

The chief instrument of the National State is Megalopolis, its biggest city, the place where the idolum of the National Utopia was first created, and where it is perpetually willed into existence.

In order to grasp the quintessential character of Megalopolis we must shut our eyes to the palpable earth, with its mantle of vegetation and its tent of clouds, and conceive what might be made of the human landscape if it could be entirely fabricated out of paper; for the ultimate aim of the Megalopolis is to conduct the whole of human life and intercourse through the medium of paper.

The early life of a young citizen in Megalopolis is spent in acquiring the tools by which paper may be used. The names of these tools are writing, reading, and arithmetic; and once upon a time these constituted the main elements in every Megalopolitan's education. There was, however, a good deal of dissatisfaction, on paper, against this somewhat barren curriculum, and so at a fairly early date in the history of Megalopolis, various other subjects, such as literature, science, gymnastics, and manual training were added to the curriculum—on paper. It is indeed possible for a Megalopolitan student to know the atomic formula of clay without ever having seen it in the raw earth, to handle pine wood in the workshop without having walked through a pine forest, and to go through the masterpieces of poetic literature without having experienced a single emotion which would prepare him to appreciate anything different from one of the influential Megalopolitan magazines, "Smutty Stories", but as long as his hours of attendance can be recorded on paper, and as long as he can give a satisfactory account of his studies on an examination paper, his preparation for life is practically complete; and so he is graduated with a paper certificate of education into the industries of Coketown, or into the multitudinous bureaus of Megalopolis itself.

The end of this period of paper tutelage is but a prelude to its continuation in another form; for the religious care of paper is the Megalopolitan's life work. The daily newspaper, the ledger, the card index are the means by which he now makes contact with life, whilst the fiction magazine and the illustrated paper are the means by which he escapes from it. Through the translucent form of paper known as celluloid, it has been possible to do away on the stage with flesh-and-blood people; and therefore the drama of life, as the Megalopolitan story writers tell it, can be enacted at one remove from actuality. Instead of his travelling, the world moves before the Megalopolitan, on paper; instead of his venturing forth on the highways of the world, adventure comes to him, on paper; instead of his getting him a mate, his bliss may be all but consummated—on paper. In fact, so accustomed does the Megalopolitan become to experiencing all his emotions on paper that he can be entertained by the representation of a static bowl of flowers on a moving picture screen; while his cockney ignorance of nature is so vast that a certain vaudeville performer, seeking to amuse him by imitating the calls of birds and beasts, finds it wise to have moving pictures taken of the rooster, the dog, and the cat, in order to give his mimicries reality in minds destitute of any personal image.

The notion of direct action, direct intercourse, direct association, is a foreign one to Megalopolis. If any action is to be taken by the whole community, or by any group in it, it is necessary to carry it through the Megalopolitan parliament, and have it established on paper, after innumerable people, who have no genuine concern in the matter, have committed their views about it to paper. If any intercourse is to be carried on, it must be largely conducted on paper; and if that medium is not directly available, subsidiary instruments, like the telephone, are used. The chief form of association in Megalopolis is that by political party, and it is through the political party that the Megalopolitan expresses his views, on paper, as to what is necessary to amend the paper constitution or promote the welfare of the paper community; albeit he realizes that the promises made by political parties are written on what Megalopolitans in their more cynical moments call "non-negotiable" paper, and will probably never pass into currency.

By its traffic in Coketown's multifarious goods and by its command over certain kinds of paper known as mortgages or securities, Megalopolis ensures a supply of real foods and real staples from the countryside. Through incessant production of books, magazines, newspapers, boilerplate features, and syndicated matter, Megalopolis ensures that the idolum of the National Utopia shall be kept alive in the minds of the underlying inhabitants of the country. Finally, by the devices of "national education" and "national advertising" all the inhabitants of the National Utopia are persuaded that the good life is that which is lived, on paper, in the capital city; and that an approximation to this life can be achieved only by eating the food, dressing in the clothes, holding the opinions, and purchasing the goods which are offered for sale by Megalopolis. So the chief aim of every other city in the National Utopia is to become like Megalopolis; its chief hope is to grow as big as Megalopolis; its boast is that it is another Megalopolis. When the denizens of Megalopolis dream of a better world, it is only a paper perfection of that National Utopia which Edward Bellamy looked forward to in Looking Backward.

Working in connection with the Machine Process of Coketown, the Megalopolis erects a standard of life which can be expressed in commercial terms, on paper, even if it does not offer any tangible satisfaction in goods and services and perfections. The chief boast of this standard is its uniformity; that is, its equal applicability to every person in the community without respect to his history, his circumstances, his needs, his actual rewards. Hence such goods as Megalopolis creates in profusion are for the most part in the line of plumbing and sanitary devices which, if they do not exactly heighten the joy of living, at any rate make the routine of Megalopolitan life a little less formidable.

The total result of these standards and uniformities is that what was originally a fiction in time becomes a fact. Whereas the inhabitants of the national utopia may originally have been as diverse as the trees in a forest, they tend to become, under the influence of education and propaganda, as similar as telegraph

[229]

poles along a road. It is not a little to the credit of Megalopolis that the National Utopia has pragmatically justified itself. It has created the sort of mental environment on paper which is necessary to a smooth adjustment of Coketown and the Country House. What is Megalopolis, in fact, but a paper purgatory which serves as a medium through which the fallen sons of Coketown, the producer's hell, may finally attain the high bliss of the Country House, the consumer's Heaven?

13

It should be plain that in describing the National Utopia and Megalopolis I have been trying to outline what Plato would call the pure form. It is equally clear, I trust, that the pure form is an idolum to which any existing national state or metropolis approximates only so far as the idolum does not conflict too grossly with the real men and women, the real communities, the real regions, the real workaday occupations which continue, despite the reign of these idola, to exist, and to occupy our main attention. Formal education has not altogether taken the place of vital education; loyalty to the state has not altogether succeeded as a substitute for deeper allegiances and affiliations: occasionally, here and there, people meet each other face to face, they eat real food, dig in real earth, smell real flowers instead of coal tar perfumes that arise from paper bouquets, and embark quite madly on real love affairs. It is true that these realities are a disturbing influence: they are always threatening to undermine the idola which the politicians and journalists and academic handymen unite so valiantly to build up; but there they are—and even the most stubborn idealist cannot help himself from occasionally confronting the world that he denies!

If you and I were perfect citizens of Megalopolis, we should never let anything come between us and our loyalty to the State: when the State called for our taxes, we should never think regretfully of the amusements we must forego in order to pay them; when the State demanded that we go to war, nothing like the claims of a family or an occupation or a moral conviction would ever step between us and our national duty. By the same token, we should never eat any other food than that which had been nationally advertized, and never buy anything direct from the producer when we might buy it from a third person in Megalopolis; we should never read any literature that is not produced in our own country, never desire any other climate than our own country can boast, and never seek to find in any other culture, remote in space or time, the things which we seem to miss in our own environment. If only this utopia of nationalism could be realized completely it would be self-sufficient; and there would be nothing on earth, in heaven, or in the waters over the earth which did not bear the authentic trademark of Megalopolis.

14

The picture of the National Utopia that I have drawn is perhaps a little too black to stand out clearly; and I must now add a few high lights for definition.

As in Coketown, there was a point up to which efficiency in mechanical production was a good thing, so in the national utopia there is a point up to which uniformity is a good thing. The National State seems historically to have arisen in some part through the relief which the people of the Middle Age experienced in being able to travel under the protection of the King's law along the King's highway, and their discovery that common laws and customs, common weights and measures, were on the whole an advantage over a multitude of senseless irregularities which continued to exist in particular neighborhoods. It was a distinct triumph for the good life when the men of London and the men of Edinburgh, let us say, realized that they had something in common as citizens of a single country, and emphasized the likenesses which bound them as men rather than the antagonisms that separated them as cities. If the National State erected barriers of trade against other countries, it at any rate broke down barriers that had long existed in even more limited regions, and that have long continued to exist in certain cities in Italy and France. So much is to the good.

But uniformity is not a good in itself. It is a good only in so far as it promotes association and social intercourse. In breaking down minor barriers, the State created major ones, and it created national uniformities in regions where they were meaningless. Moreover, nationalism is inimical to cultural unity, and it perpetuates irrelevant conflicts in the Kingdom of the Spirit where there should be neither slave nor free, neither white nor black, neither citizen nor outlander. As a matter of fact, the two great international cultural vehicles of the Middle Age—the Latin Language and the Roman Church—were broken down by the propagation of a National Language, that spoken at the National Capital, and a National Church, that which was subservient to the State; and nothing that nationalism has done since has repaired this loss. On one hand, the idolum of the National State is too narrow, because the world of culture is man's common inheritance, and not the mere segment of it which is called "national literature" or "national science." And on the other hand, the idolum is too big, for the reason that there is no bond except a paper one between men who are as far apart as Bermondsey and Bombay, or New York and San Francisco. The temporal community, as Auguste Comte finely pointed out, is local, restricted, and multiform; this is its essential nature and limitation. The spiritual community is universal. It was a great cultural misdemeanor when the National Utopia, in its extension as imperialism, sought to make the spiritual community restricted and the temporal community universal; and it is this heresy to the good life which makes all the pretensions of the national utopia so shabby and insincere.

15

If Coketown and the Country House and the National Utopia had remained on paper, they would doubtless be entertaining and edifying contributions to our literature. Unfortunately, these social myths have been potent; they have given a pattern to our lives; and they are the source of a great many evils that threaten, like stinking weeds, to choke the good life in our communities. It is not because these myths are utopias that I have been criticizing them so assiduously; it is rather because they continue to work such wholesale damage. Hence it has seemed worth while to point out that they are on pretty much the same level of reality

[233]

as the Republic or Christianopolis. We may perhaps approach our social institutions a little more courageously when we realize how completely we ourselves have created them; and how, without our perpetual "will to believe" they would vanish like smoke in the wind.

CHAPTER ELEVEN

How we reckon up accounts with the one-sided utopias
of the partisans.

CHAPTER ELEVEN

1

THERE have been many periods when men did not think it possible to make life in the community reach much higher levels than it had attained, without working a change upon human nature. The working of this change has been one of the chief preoccupations of religion; but no one can pretend that it has met, during the historic period, with any overwhelming success. In the eighteenth century men became impatient with the ministrations of institutional religion, and sought to effect an improvement in the common life by a different method—by improving the political, economic, and social mechanisms of society.

Up to this time the only method that had seemed feasible for improving the technique of social organization was the mandate of law. Although Aristotle, for instance, predicted that slavery would come to an end on the condition that the shuttle should weave by itself and the lyre play without human hand, no one in the Greek community of his time saw very much likelihood of improvement through mechanical inventions or wholesale innovations in agriculture; and no one, apparently, concerned himself seriously with the mechanical side of affairs.

It was the same during the Middle Age. If the men of that time were not exuberantly happy over their civilization, they had the dogmatic conviction that nothing very satisfactory could come of a race that had inherited the curse of Adam—a race whose only salvation could come when its individuals were purged one by one of sin, and delivered, by the intercession of the saints and the grace of God, into a more benignly constituted afterworld. One might relieve the pressure a little if the shoe pinched, perhaps, but scarcely anyone dreamed of travelling in seven-league boots, or of establishing an Arcadia in which boots could be dispensed with. It was foolish to look for a more perfect society in a world that was rife with imperfect men.

The Renascence, as we have seen, changed all this. Presently a school of philosophers followed on the heels of the utopians who devoted themselves to preparing fairly minute plans and specifications for the social order. In the beginning, these plans were devoted to politics and criminal reform, like those of Rousseau, Beccaria, Bentham, Jefferson, Godwin, and the eighteenth century reformers generally; in the nineteenth century the main accent was economic, and a number of movements arose which could be traced back to the semi-scientific investigations of Adam Smith, Ricardo, Proudhon, Malthus, Marx, and perhaps half a dozen other thinkers of outstanding importance, among whom we should perhaps include such latter day figures as Mill, Spencer, and Henry George.

All of these thinkers have in one way or another influenced our thoughts and deflected our actions; and if one adds to this galaxy the reforming elements which remained in the churches and the missionary brotherhoods and the philanthropic organizations, we can observe, growing up in the nineteenth century, a multitude of partisan organizations and movements, each of which is strenuously bent on realizing its private and partisan utopia. It is these private and partisan utopias that I purpose to make a slight reckoning with in the present chapter; but the field is such a huge and formidable one that I shall limit my criticism in the main to those that attempted to effect a change in the economic order.

2

For all the activities that men engage in we have separate words. This is a great misfortune; for in using these words we tend to believe that each action takes place in a separate compartment. Instead of beginning with a whole man interacting in a whole community, we are likely to consider only a partial man in a partial community, and by a mental sleight of hand, before we know it, we have let the part stand for the whole. It is this sort of abstraction, I believe, that has been responsible for a good deal of fallacious thinking with regard to the place of industry in the community. The economists seem to have made the error first by talking of a creature whom they called the Economic Man, a creature who had no instincts but those of construction and acquisition, no habits but of working and saving, and no other ultimate purpose than to become such a captain of industry as would make him a candidate for the biographic sketches of Mr. Samuel Smiles, and his present successors in the newspapers and popular magazines.

Now this Economic Man was the embodiment of honest labor and rapacious greed. Out of the better quality, Karl Marx painted the picture of the faithful

[239]

laborer in Coketown whose masters swindled him out of the "surplus value" he produced; out of the worse quality classical economists like Ricardo painted an equally entrancing picture of the beneficent capitalist, through whose foresight, organizing ability, and boldness business could be conducted on a scale a simpler age had scarcely dreamed of. It was out of these conceptions, as they were elaborated and rationalized in books like Porter's Progress of the Nineteenth Century and Marx's Capital, that there grew up the notion that the only fundamental problem in the modern world was the labor problem——the problem as to who should control industry, who should profit by its advances, and who should own the complicated instruments by which it was conducted.

Our business here is not to examine the various programs that were offered during the last century in answer to these problems; merely to catalog them with the barest explanation of their purpose would be an imposing task, were it not for the fact that it has been neatly done for us by Mr. Savel Zimand. It is enough to see here the common element in capitalism, copartnery, State Socialism, Guild Socialism, Co-operation, Communism, Syndicalism, the One Big Union, Trades Unionism, and the like; whether these movements represent actual facts, like capitalism, copartnery, or trades unionism, or whether they are simply projections, like Syndicalism and the One Big Union.

If our excursion through the classic utopias has been of any use, it must have shown us how pathetic is this notion that the key to a good society rests simply on the ownership and control of the industrial plant of the community. Is it any less absurd when we confess that

[240]

most of the movements which were founded upon this
assumption were actuated by generous and humane
motives, and that Francis Place, the tailor of Charing
Cross, who believed in a radical application of laissez
faire principles, was just as sincere a believer in the
common weal as Karl Marx, who predicted a dictatorship of the proletariat? If a great many of these programs have had the notion that industrial machinery,
under socialism or guildism or co-operation was to be
used for the common benefit, what was lacking was any
common notion as to what the common benefit was.

All that was common to these partisan utopias was
a desire to get rid of positive evils such as overwork or
starvation or irregularity of employment. In their
rejection of the existing order of Coketown, with its
rubbish heaps for the disposal of material waste, and
its jails, hospitals, sanatoria, doss houses, Salvation
Army Headquarters, and charitable organizations for
the disposal of the human excrement of industrialism—
in turning their backs upon these things and asserting
the simple elements of human dignity, all our radical
programs were right and inevitable. To reject what
industrial society had to offer its members in the filthy
factory districts and wretched slums of Coketown was
obviously to reject barbarism and degradation of the
worst sort: the incredible thing about the industrial
revolution, indeed, is not that there were a few riots
here and there against the use of machinery, but that
the industrial population has not been in a state of
continual insurrection, and that the industrial towns
have not been looted and razed again and again. It is
nothing less than a tribute to the fundamental good
nature and sweetness of human beings that the strikes

by which the workers have expressed their sense of grievance have not demolished the material hovels that today stand upright in the valleys of York-Riding, in the valleys of the Ohio and its tributaries, or in that terrible slum which stretches in back of the Jersey meadows from Elizabeth into Patterson. There are many districts in these areas which are scarcely worth the respect of orderly demolition. To give a grim rejection to the society that produced them only mildly meets the situation. They should be destroyed by trumpets and God's wrath—like Jericho!

So much for what is sound and valid in the various one-sided programs for reform. But if their attitude towards the past performances of industrialism was sound, their gesture towards the future, and their attitude towards the whole milieu, was little less than indifferent. There were to be certain gains in money wages, in political control, in the distribution of products, and so forth; but the realization of these gains was never projected in any very vivid way—a vague fellowship in peace and plenty under gay red banners was all that was left over when the current efforts to "educate the masses," "revise the constitution," or "organize the revolution" were taken for granted.

In his Socialism: Utopian and Scientific, Friedrich Engels made a plea for a realistic method of thought, which limited itself to a here and now, as against what he derided as the utopian method, the attempt on the part of a single thinker to give a detailed picture of the society of the future. Yet at the present time it is easy to see that if the utopian socialism of Owen has been ineffective, the realistic socialism of Marx has been equally ineffective; for while Owen's kind of socialism

[242]

has been partly fulfilled in the co-operative movement, the dictatorship of the proletariat rests upon very shaky foundations, and such success as it has had is due perhaps as much to Marx's literary picture of what it would be like as to anything else. I do not doubt that the partisan movements have achieved many specific gains; consumer's co-operation alone has in England measurably lightened the physical burden of existence for a great many people. Their weakness consists in the fact that they have not altered the contents of the modern social order, even when they have altered the method of distribution; and in addition, a good many of these partisan utopias, for lack of any definite and coherent scheme of values, crumble away as soon as they meet the opposition of such powerful collective utopias as Coketown or the Country House. In America, particularly, the labor movement is paralyzed by this perpetual movement into the bourgeoisie—concretely speaking, into Suburbia and the Country House —and in Great Britain much the same sort of dereliction can be observed within the narrower group from which the leaders of the trades unions and the Labor Party are drawn.

Hence also the less interesting problem of the Tired Radical, which Mr. Walter Weyl suggestively outlined. There is indeed a pertinent criticism of the paper environment of Megalopolis, in the tenacious way in which people continue to cling to abstract programs and to movements which never approach perceptibly nearer their fulfillment. The marvel is that the concrete utopia of the Country House has not exercised a more potent influence than it actually does. When one compares the vast amount of agitation during the last century—the Chartist Movement, the Socialist Movement, the International Peace Movement—with the actual results in the reconstruction of work, place, and people, or with the actual effects any reconstruction has had upon our polity, our culture, our art—it is surprising that these movements have had any effective claim upon our allegiance. Men will indeed work for an idea—the notion that they will not is a superstition—but sooner or later the spirit must be made manifest in the flesh, and if it never comes to birth, or at best is an abortion, the idea is bound to wither away.

How long would the parliamentary clatter of socialism have mechanically kept on—had it not been for the dislocation of war? How long could its abstract programs have remained in the air, before coming down to specifications? I obviously cannot answer these questions; but it seems plain enough that our radical programs have had simply a sentimental interest: they moved people without giving them a specific task, they stirred them emotionally without giving them an outlet, and so, at best, they are but partial utopias of escape, using the powers of organization, collective meetings, and pronunciamentos to take the place of the emotional stimuli which the avowed utopia of escape, like News from Nowhere, supplies by introducing a beautiful girl. In this aspect, the Socialist Party, with its revolutionary demands, did not differ in its psychological performance from the Republican Party, which specialized in the rhetorical device of the full dinner pail; nor did it differ in any fundamental way from the defunct Progressive Party, which for a time believed in a new heaven and earth to follow the initia-

[244]

tive, referendum, and recall with an intensity of moral conviction beside which the social revolutionist was positively tame.

Who doubts the honesty and sincerity of most of the members of these parties? Who doubts their devotion to revolution or "uplift"? It is all beside the point. A machine which doesn't work because it is badly constructed is just as useless as one that doesn't work because its maker is a deliberate fraud; and all the sincerity and good will and honesty doesn't make any one a smile the happier. It is about time that we faced the facts and realized that in all our sundry mechanisms of reform "there is a screw loose somewhere." This pregnant metaphor of the industrial age is usually applied to neurotic disorder; and I am using it in the present context with fell intentions. I mean that the utopia of the partisan is, psychologically speaking, a fetish; that is to say, it is an attempt to substitute the part for the whole, and to pour into the part all the emotional content that belongs to the whole. When a man gets hold of a lady's handkerchief or garter, and behaves towards that object with as much intensity and interest as he would towards its flesh and blood owner, the handkerchief or garter is said to be a fetish. I hazard the judgment that Socialism, Prohibition, Proportional Representation, and the various other abstract "isms" are the fetishes of the partisan: they are attempts to make some particular instrument or function of the community stand for the whole. It is doubtless much easier to filch a handkerchief than to win a girl. By the same token, it is easier to concentrate on the use of liquor or the ownership of machinery and land than upon the totality of

[245]

a community's activities. It is easier indeed; but it is fatal; for the result of this fetishism is perhaps that the girl remains unmated, and the society fails to undergo any fundamental change. Moreover, the reforming elements in society become incapacitated by their practice of fetishism to take a normal part in the community's activities; and remain so much waste material—at best, they wander between two worlds, "one dead, the other powerless to be born."

We know these disoriented reformers, these disillusioned revolutionaries, these tired radicals; we could mention names if it were not so needless and so cruel. Apart from anything else, their original mistake was to keep their problem within the compartment of politics and economics, instead of venting it to the wide world. They forgot that the adjustment of some single activity or institution, without respect to the rest, begged the very difficulty they were trying to overcome. If they were anti-militarists, they saw the world simply as an armed camp; if they were socialists, they saw it as a gigantic mechanism of exploitation; and alas! they saw only so much of the world as would conveniently fit within these diagrams. The world is perhaps an armed camp and a mechanism of exploitation; it is all that and much more; but any attempt to deal with it on a wholesale plan by eliminating all the qualifying elements in the problem is bound to encounter the brute nature of things; and if the nature of things is essentially antagonistic, the reform itself will fail.

To say all this is to emphasize the obvious. If any further emphasis were needed it would be necessary only to compare the doctrines of Marx, as expounded by Lenin at the beginning of the Russian Revolution, and the doctrines of Lenin, as tempered by experience and circumstance a few years later.

3

There was still another weakness that characterized all the partisan utopias of the nineteenth century. That weakness was their externalism.

If the mediæval thinkers were convinced that, on the whole, nothing could be done to rectify men's institutions, while men themselves were so easily bitten by corruption, their successors in the nineteenth century committed the opposite kind of error and absurdity: they believed that human nature was unsocial and obstreperous only because the church, the state, or the institution of property perverted every human impulse. Men like Rousseau, Bentham, Godwin, Fourier, and Owen might be miles apart from one another in their criticism of society, but there was an underlying consensus in their belief in human nature. They looked upon human institutions as altogether external to men; these were so many straitjackets that cunning rulers had thrown over the community to make sane and kindly people behave like madmen; and they could conceive of changing the institutions without changing the habits and redirecting the impulses of the people by whom and for whom they had been created. If one devised neat political constitutions, with plenty of checks and balances, or laid out pauper colonies and invited the countryside to make use of them—well, all would be to the good.

There was, it is true, one great exception to this notion that institutions might be reformed without, in that process, making over men. I refer to the belief in education which accompanied these classic criticisms of human institutions; for this seems to point to a perception that men needed a special training and discipline before they could enter freely into the life of a reconstituted community. But upon examination, this exception melts away. The emphasis in the new programs of education was upon the formal, institutional acquirement of the apparatus of knowledge; and they, too, began with the clean slate of a new generation, whereas the critical difficulty was that of getting the adult community sufficiently educated, in a realistic sense, to be able to make over its educational institutions; and in this respect the reformers were just as much in Cuckooland as—well, Campanella. So it follows that the Country House and Coketown shared honors in building up the new educational organizations; and the outcome of the sort of education that the public school and college provided was to make these redoubtable utopias practically unassailable.

Besides, there were the adults: consider Robert Owen!

Robert Owen, one of the most sanguine advocates of popular education, was himself a living example of the need for a different kind of discipline than his narrow and homiletic mind, with its childish interpretation of religious belief and its equally childish rationalism, was capable of framing. No one ever frustrated so many good ideas, from the plan of garden cities down to the project for co-operative production than this same Owen, whose bumptiousness, arrogance, and conceit were bound to provoke reactions in other people which would have defeated the plans of Omnipotence itself. The capital difficulty was to get any sort of social improvement in a world that was full of refractory Owens. A locomotive may, in a sense, be a more perfect thing than the man who made it; but no social order can be better than the human beings who take part in it; for whereas the locomotive can stand apart from its operatives and perform all its functions effectively even if the workers themselves are deficient in every other respect than mechanics, with a social order the product and the producer continue to be one.

Not merely does a community need a Buddha, let us say, before it can produce Buddhism; it needs a whole succession of Buddhas if the religion itself is not to fritter away into the hideous ecclesiastical grind it became in Thibet. This principle has a general application. The social critics of the last century confused the mechanical problem of transforming an institution or of creating a new organization with the personal and social problem of spurring people to effect the transformation and see it through. Their tactics were those of a general who would go into battle without training his army; their strategy was that of the demagogue who talks of a million armed men springing up overnight. The personal problem, the problem of education, was as easy as that!

If we are to account for the poverty of our achievements in renovating the community, in contrast with the enormous amount of quite justifiable economic and political agitation, research, and criticism, it is perhaps not altogether fair to put the entire burden of failure upon the partisan's lop-sided utopia. The plans of our reformers have indeed been weak and jerrybuilt in themselves; but that is not all. What has perhaps been even more conspicuously lacking has been people who are accessible to the existing knowledge, people whose minds have been trained to play freely with the facts, people who have learned the fine and exacting art of co-operating with their fellows; people who are as critical of their own mental processes and habits of behavior as they are of the institutions they wish to alter. As Viola Paget says: "The bulk of thinking and feeling intended to help on human improvement has not really been good enough for the purpose. Not good enough in the sense of not sufficiently impersonal and disciplined."

Between our programs, our utopias, and their fulfillment there has usually dropt a thick veil of personalities; and were the plan itself the collaborate product of the best minds of the race; as Mr. H. G. Wells satirically pictured in Boon, it would still have to take its chances with the wild asses of the devil that human weakness, apathy, greed, lust for power, might release. Walt Whitman said of Carlyle that behind the tally of his work and genius stood the stomach, and gave a sort of casting vote. So one may say of every social movement, that behind the tally of its theoretic background and its concrete programs stand human beings—hale and sick, neurotic and stable, well-intentioned and malicious—and give the casting vote.

Anyone who has read an important book, and then met the author, who has respected an apparently significant social movement, and then met the leaders behind the scenes, will realize how frequent is the difficulty of reconciling theoretic agreement with the inaccessibilities and prejudices and repugnances of particular personalities. No one can join the work of even the most trivial sort of committee—be it a delegation to

[250]

shake hands with the Congressman or a body designated to revise the rules of a tennis club—without discovering how the work in hand is perpetually being balked and diverted by the play of personalities.

It is not a little significant that popular speech gives the word "personalities" a derogatory meaning. Again and again the success or failure in large collaborations hinges upon human factors that have no bearing on the question at issue. Pope's satiric words about wretches hanging that jurymen may dine touches the point neatly. Our programs for reconstruction that have not reckoned with the perpetual cussedness of human nature and have no method for exorcising it are as shallow as those older theologies which sought to make men live in grace without altering the social order in which they functioned. Perhaps they could learn something from the story of that ancient agitator who cured the blind, the maimed, the sick, and the halt before he bade them enter into the Kingdom of Heaven. Emerson well said in his essay on Man the Reformer that it was stupid to expect any real or permanent change from any social program which was unable to regenerate or convert—these are religious phases for a common psychological phenomenon—the people who are to engineer it and carry it through.

It would be so easy, this business of making over the world, if it were only a matter of creating machinery. There has probably never been lacking the sort of energy and talent that is needed for this sort of work; and at any rate, during the last three centuries, with the growth of technology, the mechanical services at the command of our engineers and organizers are huge and adequate. Unfortunately, we are still in the same ditch that Carlyle mordantly pointed out in his essay on Characteristics: Given a world of knaves, we are trying by various cunning devices to produce an honesty from their united action. I do not share Carlyle's contempt for human nature in the raw, but he is quite right, I believe, in making fun of the superficiality of our partisan utopias. These utopias were so concerned to alter the shell of the community's institutions that they neglected to pay attention to the habits of the creature itself—or its habitat. That is why mechanical devices play such an important part, perhaps, in all these utopias, from Jeremy Bentham, with his Panopticon method of reforming criminals, down to the hideous cog-and-wheel utopia of Edward Bellamy.

The conceptions of human life that our reforming groups have had have been pretty thin and unsatisfying. Any adequate conception of a new social order would, it seems to me, include the scenery, the actors, and the play. It is a mark of our immaturity that we never seem able to get beyond the scene shifting. Our social theorists, in so far as they consider the actors at all, are inclined to treat them as mechanical puppets. As for the play itself—the universal drama of courtship and trial and adventure and contest and achievement, in which every human being is potentially the hero or heroine—the play itself has hardly entered into their consciousness. Their values have not been human values: they have been such values as have been authenticated by commerce and industry, values such as efficiency, fair wages, and what not. These, at any rate, have been the immediate objects of effort, and if human values hung vaguely in the background, they were to be realized in a distant and unascertainable future. So

one often feels that no matter how base and deteri-
orated the modern community is, it nevertheless retains
in its totality a greater measure of human values than
many of the groups that have attacked its inadequacy
have to offer.

All this comes out pretty plainly in the attitude of
the labor groups towards the current situation.
Whether they are organized for political action or for
industrial warfare, their aims are curiously similar.
In the very act of contending against the present order,
they have accepted the ends for which that order stands
and have been content to demand simply that they be
universalized. This perhaps accounts for the essential
uncreativeness of the labor movement. By a revolution
they do not mean a transvaluation of values: they mean
a dilution and spreading out of established practices
and institutions. There may indeed be plenty of excuse for this attitude in any particular situation—a
group of unorganized and semi-destitute workers such
as those in many American steel plants—but the worst
of it is that this attitude characterizes the more advanced and economically secure groups, and creeps into
such ultimate programs as one can deduce from attempts to create workers' educational institutions—
as if a change in ownership or the balance of power
would alter the face of Coketown so that its fires would
no longer burn and its cinders no longer smut.

I have emphasized what is the weakness, as it seems
to me, of the labor movement; not because I am necessarily out of sympathy with any particular measure
that might be proposed, but because it illustrates upon
an enormous scale the point which I desire to make.
The prohibition movement, or the charity organiza-

tion movement—towards both of which I feel, on the contrary, a cordial antipathy—would serve just as well for illustration; for they all have this common distinction: they lack any explicit, consciously projected humane ends which would make any particular measure that they might offer justified.

4

Let me now anticipate the answer which this criticism will probably meet. To some people it will seem that the current movements for reform are inevitably secular; that they have no business to concern themselves with the ultimate faith of men; that they inevitably deal with a limited here and now, a dollar more of wages, a drop less of liquor, a touch more of uniformity, and so forth. In short, our partial utopias need not concern themselves with any of the questions that have to do with the life of the spirit.

The simple answer to this crude philosophy is—so much the worse for them. The breach between the institutions that deal with the material life and those that deal with the ideal life results either in a complete dissociation, by which each set of institutions becomes paralytic and imbecile; or, as so often happens, in a capitulation of the spiritual power to the temporal, and its complete engrossment in temporal ends. I am aware that these phrases, "spiritual" and "temporal," have a certain old-fashioned smell; but they precisely express my meaning: it is plain that every community contains the corresponding institutions—one group being devoted to values and the other to means. When our reforms are not touched by a sense of values, the result is that purely temporal ends are taken as ultimate, and we have such notions as efficiency or organization regarded as the very touchstone of social improvement. This is scarcely an improvement over the old order of things, with which we are now so dismally familiar—the state in which our values were not fertilized by any intercourse with the concrete and actual world about us, and so remained remote and sterile. In short, unless our reformers concern themselves with the ultimate values of men, with what constitutes a good life, they are bound to pander to such immediate faiths and superstitions as the National State, Efficiency, or the White Man's Burden.

5

There is a final criticism of the partial utopias: our one-sided reforms have had this fatal defect—they are one-sided. This partisanship was expressed by their relation to the facts upon which their programs were based, and in their attitude towards the people who were to be affected by them.

The mood of partisanship has been that of a lawyer who is getting up an argument and is looking for such facts as will bolster up his case. That mood is inimical to free and intelligent thought: its object is rhetorical triumph. Now it happens that in all the matters which intimately concern a community, a person's attitude towards the facts not merely seems more important than the facts themselves, but seems so deucedly important that the facts are ignored. The attitude of a group of Southern whites who will lynch a negro on the report that he has raped a white woman before they investigate the truth of the assertion is a bestial exaggeration of a very natural human tendency. Men are built for action rather than thought; or rather, since thought, on the psychologist's interpretation, is inhibited action, the business of inhibition naturally comes a little hard to us; and when we are in a place where we have the rough choice of pushing through the obstacle, under a strong impulse of resentment (instinct of pugnacity) or may quietly withdraw from the obstacle, survey it, and frame a plan of action to circumvent it, our fundamental impulse is to follow the first mode.

It is easy to see, for example, how the hideous human suffering which accompanied the growth of the capitalist organization—and still exists!—caused the socialists to concentrate attention upon the subjects of ownership and profits, and long blinded them to the specific problems of organization, distribution, and control within the industries that might be affected by the program of socialization. This concentration upon the particular aspect of a problem, like the concentration upon a particular aspect of the solution, has the weakness of ignoring the total situation, and it too crudely simplifies the difficulties. In their haste to arrive at solutions and remedies—for the life of man is short and the needs of the moment are pressing—the partisans neglect to make a complete tally of the facts; and they are too ready to let "common knowledge" take the place of a thorough investigation of the data.

This weakness arises out of an almost instinctive tendency towards partisanship; and it is one of the reasons that partisanship continues. If nothing else prevents groups from getting together, their failure to agree about the facts, and their lack of a method for getting at the facts and focussing them, is responsible. If an examination of the facts did nothing else, it might

[256]

show at least the impossibility of drawing any conclusion from them, and it might warn the partisan to step warily. Thus the testimony that was offered for and against Prohibition came from fairly high authorities on both sides; and if there had been anything like right reason in the strategically stronger camp, it would have convinced those who were interested in the welfare of the community that nothing could be wisely done while the very basis for judgment—scientific knowledge as to the place of alcoholic stimuli in the life of the human organism—had not been established.

It is of course conceivable that men will quarrel and split when they are fully apprised of the facts: we may well remember the story of the British ambassador who confessed to his French colleague that the reason he did not get on very well with the Americans was that both countries unfortunately spoke the same language; but it is inconceivable that they should ever reach an intelligent agreement before they are in common possession of the facts. By ignoring the necessity for substantiating his claims and assertions the partisan frequently not merely fails to see his whole problem in all its implications, but also prevents any one else from seeing it. Even when the partisan is not intentionally blind, he lacks the discipline which is essential to an open-eyed judgment of the case. What that discipline may be I shall attempt to discuss in the next chapter.

The second weakness of partisanship is that it breaks the community into vertical divisions, and promotes fictitious antagonisms and kinships which run against the horizontal affiliations and loyalties of a man's life. This tendency was nicely illustrated in a play by Mr. St. John Ervine, called Mixed Marriage, which dealt

[257]

with the love affair of a young girl and a young man who were separated by the religions that had been handed down by their parents. In Mr. Ervine's wretched little Ulster community, these religions served as an excuse to keep people from being friendly and decent to their neighbors. Now it is obvious that mating, and making friends with those who have common interests and sentiments, and mixing freely within the whole community, are highly important horizontal interests; they tend to unite people in a common bond which is fundamental for the reason that these interests and activities are essentially human. The antagonism between two Christian sects, on the other hand, undermines the good life as a whole, because it insists that there is no other good than a religious good—a good embodied in a pope, or in the practice of scoffing at a pope—while it is obvious to anyone who has possession of his senses that kissing a pretty girl is good, and having a friendly pipe with one's neighbor is good, and that institutions which prevent one from doing these things at appropriate times are perverted and antisocial. It is true that people who emphasize religious interests take "high ground," as the saying is, and that those who value the friendly pipe seem by implication to take low ground: but what the partisans fail to see is that there is a good human case for low ground, and that, for the great majority of people it may prove to be not merely the only practicable ground, but in its own right a good and sufficient one.

Now for Catholic and Protestant in Mr. St. John Ervine's play one may substitute Democrat and Republican, White Guard and Red Guard, Socialist and Financier, Prohibitionist and anti-Prohibitionist and the results will be just as deplorably the same. There are any number of interests in a well-wrought life which lie altogether beyond these categories, and it is the chief misdemeanor of partisanism, as opposed to utopianism, that it tends to slight these general interests, and either bring them into the service of the "ism" or urge that they be neglected in devotion to the "cause." The first method has been used by the apostles of nationalism. The National State, recognizing that art and culture and science could not be altogether engrossed in the strategy of political warfare, promptly put these goods in the pigeon hole labelled national resources. The partisans of the State talked about American science as opposed to German science, of Italian art as opposed to French art; and thus emphasized the things which men in America had with other Americans in order to mark off more clearly the things they had apart from men of similar interests in other countries. The same thing happened in the Russian communist state, with its attempt to set aside the common cultural heritage of mankind at large and define a purely proletarian culture. The results in every case are, I believe, incurably mischievous; and those who would promote the good life must cease this infantile practice of asserting vainly that "my father knows more than your father," "my mother is more beautiful than your mother"—and so on.

For the most part the second method has been indefatigably used. In the political state the partisans make a great show of the gulf which separates the political party in power from that which is outside, and every other interest in life is supposed to be secondary to this abysmal cleavage. In relatively crude communities, like the United States and Ireland, these differences seem to be taken by the great mass of people at their face value; whereas in England, which at least has the virtues of disillusion, it is the great tradition of Parliament that all the animosities of the floor are ignored in the bar of the House of Commons, while all the congenialities and convivialities that bind men together are emphasized. Lest I be accused of prejudice where none exists, let me add that in the most substantial reconstruction movement that Ireland possesses— I refer to agricultural co-operation as promoted by Sir Horace Plunkett and A. E.—the horizontal interests which bind men together as farmers and members of a local community are successfully emphasized to the exclusion of irrelevant vertical differences, at least in matters touching the organization and conduct of the Irish Agricultural Organization Society; and that, as far as I can see, this single organization has done more to promote the good life in Ireland than any other institution, with the possible exception of the equally non-partisan literary association which grew up in Dublin under the leadership of A. E., William Butler Yeats, Lady Gregory, and the rest of that fine and glorious crew.

Obviously, it is not altogether for nothing that men have joined together in vertical organizations which are as broad as a continent, let us say, or the European world. There is a sense in which the Christians of Jerusalem have more in common with the Christians of Rome than they have with the Jews and Mohammedans of their local region. In the same way, I find myself more deeply drawn to certain friends of mine in Bombay and London than I am towards my next

[260]

door neighbor, with whom the only recognizable bond is our common animus against a rapacious landlord. So long as the vertical affiliation with people of the same views in politics or religion or philosophy is a spiritual affiliation a great deal of good may come out of it. When, however, the things that draw people together as members of a vertical group are used as a means of inflicting similar opinions or practices upon the local community, without respect to its regional qualities, the results are little less than disastrous. The rain falls on the just and the unjust; more than that, the food that we grow, the houses that we build, the roads that we lay down, the thoughts that we think, belong to us as members of the human species who have inherited the earth and the fullness thereof; and it is absurd to let differences in our idola prevent us from participating equally in this common heritage.

At long last, the things that unite human beings as human beings, the social inheritance that enables them to realize their stature as human beings, are more important than any particular element that the partisan may lay hold of. Whether our partisanism consists in being first and foremost an American or first and foremost a Theosophist, it tends to limit the world with which we may have commerce and so impoverishes the personality. The person who insists upon being a hundred per cent. American has by that very emphasis become something less than half a man. By fastening attention upon a segment of the world, the partisan creates a segment of a personality. It is these segments or sects that any movement which aims at a general good in the community must contend against. So long as work for the common welfare meets with

[261]

irrelevant partisanisms, so long will we lack the means of creating whole men and women; and so long will the main concerns of civilization be side-tracked:

6

What a vision these partisan utopias present! They are like the scattered bones that the prophet saw in the terrible valley, and one doubts whether even the breath of the Lord could knit them together again into real bodies. . . .

One of these partisan utopias issues from a bundle of red-tape; everything is filed and ticketed and labelled there; and anything in life that cannot be treated in this fashion does not exist. Another is a mechanical contraption; somehow it seems to litter little mechanical contraptions; and its aim is, it would seem, to do away with vegetation and reproduction, so that everything under the sun might be performed with the sterile accuracy of the machine. A third utopia of the partisan calls human beings, with all their color and thickness, "individuals," and makes the good life a matter of legal relationships without any regard to their necessities in time and space; such a utopia could almost be carried in one's pocket, so much is it a matter of verbal statement. We need not go down the line. Singly, it is plain that not one of these utopias would create a happy community; while if all of these partisanisms could be realized the result could scarcely be anything else than discord—such a discord as now exists and every day becomes more raucous.

It would seem that we are at an impasse. Even if I have absurdly exaggerated the futility of the reformers and revolutionaries, their lack of any fundamental program and their inability to conceive an essential reorientation in modern society, come out pretty plainly. If our analysis did not prove this, the atmosphere of disillusion which we breathe today, and which permeates every branch of literature, would tell as much. In so far as we have accepted the modern social order we are in ruin; and the next war that now threatens will, if it actually comes to pass, only carry the ruin a little further. In so far as we have pinned our hopes to current movements for reconstruction or revolution, our plans are sickly and debilitated. In fact, the only genuine signs of life seem to be in regions like Ireland, Denmark, India, and China, which have stood outside the movement of industrial civilization and have retained the values of an order which elsewhere has been undermined and almost destroyed. It is not a pretty situation to face; and small wonder that we are so slow and so reluctant to face it. Whichever way we look, bankruptcy seems to threaten us.

It is time we endeavored to cash in the paper roubles of the partisan. If our civilization is to hold together we must place its intellectual currency on a new basis; we must exchange our abstract idealisms, our abstract programs, our paperized pursuit of happiness for some of the golden coinage of life, even though we cannot have our gold without mixing it with baser metals.

CHAPTER TWELVE

How the half-worlds go, and how eutopia may come;
and what we need before we can build Jerusalem in
any green and pleasant land.

CHAPTER TWELVE

1

THE sort of thinking that has created our utopias has placed desire above reality; and so their chief fulfillment has been in the realm of fantasy. This is true of the classic utopias that we have surveyed, and it is true—though not perhaps quite so apparent—of the partial utopias that were formulated by the various reconstruction movements during the last century.

While the classic utopias have so far been nearer to reality that they have projected a whole community, living and working and mating and spanning the gamut of man's activity, their projections have nevertheless been literally up in the air, since they did not usually arise out of any real environment or attempt to meet the conditions that this environment presented. This defect has been suggested by the very name of Utopia, for as Professor Patrick Geddes points out, Sir Thomas More was an inveterate punster, and Utopia is a mock-name for either Outopia, which means no-place, or Eutopia—the good place.

It is time to bring our utopian idola and our everyday world into contact; indeed, it is high time, for the idola that have so far served us are now disintegrating so rapidly that our mental world will soon be as empty of useful furniture as a deserted house, while wholesale dilapidation and ruin threaten the institutions that

seemed permanent. Unless we can weave a new
rn for our lives the outlook for our civilization is
t as dismal as Herr Spengler finds it in Der
rgang des Abendlandes. Our choice is not between
eutopia and the world as it is, but between eutopia
and nothing—or rather, nothingness. Other civilizations have proved inimical to the good life and have
failed and past away; and there is nothing but our own
will-to-eutopia to prevent us from following them.

If this dissipation of Western Civilization is to cease,
the first step in reconstruction is to make over our inner world, and to give our knowledge and our projections a new foundation. The problem of realizing the
potential powers of the community—which is the fundamental problem of eutopian reconstruction—is not
simply a matter of economics or eugenics or ethics as
the various specialist thinkers and their political followers have emphasized. Max Beer, in his History of
British Socialism, points out that Bacon looked for
the happiness of mankind chiefly in the application of
science and industry. But by now it is plain that if
this alone were sufficient, we could all live in heaven
tomorrow. Beer points out that More, on the other
hand, looked to social reform and religious ethics to
transform society; and it is equally plain that if the
souls of men could be transformed without altering
their material and institutional activities, Christianity,
Mohammedanism, and Buddhism might have created an
earthly paradise almost any time this last two thousand
years. The truth is, as Beer sees, that these two conceptions are still at war with each other: idealism and
science continue to function in separate compartments;

and yet "the happiness of man on earth" depends upon their combination.

If we are to build up genuine eutopias, instead of permitting ourselves to pattern our behavior in terms of fake utopias like Coketown, the Country House, the National State, and all the other partial and inadequate myths to which we have given allegiance, we must examine anew the idola which will assist us in reconstituting our environment. So we are forced to consider the place of science and art in our social life, and to discuss what must be done in order to make them bear more concretely upon "the improvement of man's estate."

2

There was a time when the world of knowledge and the world of dreams were not separated; when the artist and the scientist, for all practical purposes, saw the "outside world" through the same kind of spectacles.

What we call "science" today was in its primitive state part and parcel of that common stock of knowledge and belief which makes up a community's literature, or, as Dr. Beattie Crozier would have said, its "Bible." The departure of science from this main body of literature begins for the Western World, probably, with the death of Plato and the institution of Aristotle's collections in natural history; and from that point onwards the separate sciences, increasingly isolate themselves from the general body of knowledge, and utilize methods which had been unknown to the earlier philosophers and sages; so that by the time the twentieth century dawns the process of differentiation has been completed, and philosophy, once the compendium of the sciences, has disappeared except as a sort of impalpable, viscous residue.

When Aristotle divided his writing into the exoteric and esoteric groups, into the popular and the scientific, he definitely recognized the existence of two separate branches of literature, two different ways of taking account of the world, two disparate methods of approaching its problems. The first branch was that of the philosophers, the prophets, the poets, and the plain people. Its background was the generality of human experience: its methods were those of discussion and conference: its criteria were those of formal dialectics: its interests were specifically those of the community, and nothing human was foreign to it. With the petrification of Greek thought that followed the collapse of the Alexandrian school, the second branch was slow in coming into its own. As late as the eighteenth century its adherents were called natural philosophers, to distinguish them from the more humane variety; and it is only with the nineteenth century that the subject became universally known as science and its practitioners as scientists.

In the Phædrus Socrates had expressed the humanist outlook of literature by saying: "Trees and fields, you know, cannot teach me anything, but men in the city can." The shortest way of describing the attitude of science is to say that it resolutely turned its back on men in the city and devoted itself to the trees and fields and stars and the rest of brute nature. If it paid attention to men at all it saw them—if we may abuse an old quotation—as trees walking. Socrates had said: Know thyself. The scientist said: Know the world that lies outside man's dominion. As science progressed these attitudes became more rigid, unfortunately, and a conflict grew up between literature and science, between the humanities and natural philosophy, which has given both art and science the peculiar twist we shall presently examine.

Now the developments in modern science go back, through the Arabic thinkers, to ancient Greece; but the great advances that have been made date back scarcely three centuries. On the basis of the precise knowledge of physical relations which became available in mathematics, physics, mechanics, and chemistry the startling changes which have been crudely labelled the "industrial revolution" were carried through. If the essential relationship between the world of ideas and the world of action were ever in doubt, the industrial revolution, especially in its later phases, would be a final demonstration; for beneath the ostensible skyscrapers, subways, factories, telephone lines, and sewers of the modern industrial city lie the immaterial foundations of western physical science, laid down stone by stone in the remote, theoretic researches of Boyle, Faraday, Kelvin, Leibniz, and the rest of that great galaxy. With the far reaching effect of the idola of physical science it is hardly necessary to deal. Everyone realizes how dependent the advance in technology has been upon theoretic science, even though the scientist himself, as Kropotkin pointed out, is sometimes slow in admitting the debt of science itself to practical invention. The actual world of machinery is at present, it seems fair to say, a parasite upon this body of knowledge, and it would speedily starve to death if the host were annihilated.

Science has provided the factual data by means of

which the industrialist, the inventor, and the engineer
have transformed the physical world; and without
doubt the physical world has been transformed. Unfortunately, when science has furnished the data its
work is at an end: whether one uses the knowledge of
chemicals to cure a patient or to poison one's grand-
mother is, from the standpoint of science, an extraneous
and uninteresting question. So it follows that while
science has given us the means of making over the world,
the ends to which the world has been made over have
had, essentially, nothing to do with science. Accordingly, as I have suggested, the idola of the Country
House and Coketown and the National State, which
were built up by literature and art, have given the
effective direction to these transformations. So far,
science has not been used by people who regarded man
and his institutions scientifically. The application of
the scientific method to man and his institutions has
hardly been attempted.

Even when one qualifies this last generalization, its
outline remains pretty sharp. The development of
what are called the social sciences was dimly outlined
in Bacon's Novum Organon; but it was not till the
eighteenth century, with Quesnay and Montesquieu,
that the movement gained any real headway, and down
to this day a large part of what is called science in
Economics, Politics, and Sociology is only disguised
literature—work in which the jargon of science is accepted as a substitute for the scientific method of ar-
riving at factual truth, and in which the effort to mold
conduct overwhelms the attempt to reach correct conclusions. Indeed, among the economists and sociologists there has been a persistent dribble of discussion

as to whether or not their subjects entitled them to the august designation of scientists.

It is not without reason that the social and human sciences have been distrusted by the devotees of physical science, so that, for example, the British Association has long had a single section devoted to the social sciences in which Sociology, the mother of them all, is permitted to enter as a subclassification of Anthropology! The nearer the investigator gets to man, the more easily he is overwhelmed with the complexity of his subject; and the more tempted he is to adopt the swift and easy partisan methods of the novelist, the poet, the prophet. The mere concealment of this act of seduction under the rough, grey cover of scientific jargon means frequently that the social scientist has added to the offense of not being a good scientist by not even being a good literary man.

Hence there is a great gap between the more external part of the world which has been affected by science, and that part, nearer to man and man's institutions, which has yet for the greater part to be conquered. While the physical equipment of New York compares with that of fourth century Athens as Athens itself would compare with an Aurignacian cave, the life of men in the city is perhaps more disordered and futile and incomplete than the author of the Republic found it. The moral of this contrast need hardly be pointed in so many words. The idolum of science is incomplete; for it chiefly touches life in its physical sector; and it remains to complete the span so that every activity and condition may be described, measured, and grasped in scientific terms. With the vast modern improvement in our physical arrangements in view, it must occur to almost anyone that a permanent advance in social life depends upon a much more thorough and realistic acquaintance with the facts than the social sciences have yet been able to provide. Before an army moves over the land it is well for it to have moved in someone's mind over a topographic map. Lacking such maps, all our day to day improvements have been wasteful sallies into eutopia, proceeding without order, without a sufficient equipment, and without any general plan.

3

There is a point up to which each science may well be left to cultivate its field for its own sake, without any regard for the fruits. Mr. Thorstein Veblen, in The Place of Science in Civilization, has well pointed out the way in which science arises out of idle curiosity; and science, studied and advanced for its own sake, is surely one of the great playthings of the race. In this aspect, while science seeks a quite different path to the contemplative life than art takes, its end is the same—the dominant interest is an esthetic one, the joy of pure perception. Science is thus a sort of world in itself, and it is self-sufficient: there is no need for it to make contact with the real world in which we fight and love and earn our daily bread. In its own world, science is no better and no worse than theosophy or astrology or fables about deity.

But the divorce of science from the daily life of the community is not altogether an advantage. If it fosters a whole-hearted cultivation of science for its own values, it tends to lose sight of realities without which its values are meaningless. It is hard perhaps to locate the point at which science, divorced from every day realities, ceases to have any social relevance; but it seems to me that such a point exists; and when the sciences remain disparate and unrelated one to the other, they tend to pass over from a public world to the private world of the specialist; and the knowledge which obtains in that world can with difficulty be brought out again to irrigate the common life of the community; or if it is brought out, as bacteriology is brought out in relation to the treatment of disease, it is divorced from a consideration of the total situation in a way that makes so many specialist advances in medicine, for example, the stamping ground for the fanatic.

This loss of contact, I believe, is highly dangerous; for it lessens the effect of scientific discipline upon daily affairs quite as much as a cloistered religion, by erecting impossible sanctions, opens the way for much unalloyed slackness and baseness, and by demanding that Pistol and Falstaff live like Christ prevents these biological rapscallions from achieving so much as the level of Robin Hood. The upshot of this dissociation of science and social life is that superstition takes the place of science among the common run of men, as a more easily apprehended version of reality.

Today the whole corpus of knowledge is in an anarchic state, and it lacks order precisely because it lacks any definite relations to the community which creates it, and for which it, in turn, provides the spectacles through which the world is seen. Against the gains that have come from the increasing specialization of the sciences, we have to set off the losses which the community suffers from the development of crude forms of science, and from quackeries like astrology and spiritualism which succeed in giving a complete account of man's place in the universe in terms that are fairly intelligible to the lay mind. It seems to me, then, that in the cultivation of the sciences a definite hierarchy of values must be established which shall have some relation to the essential needs of the community. The independence of science from human values is a gross superstition: the desire for order, for security, for esthetically satisfactory patterns—along with the desire for fame or the favor of princes—have all played their parts in the development of science. Though the logic of science may discount the human factor as far as possible in its internal operations, it is because men have placed a certain value upon disinterested intellectual operations that these activities are pursued in modern communities to the exclusion of other interests and claims.

Let us put the problem concretely. A community which cultivates chemical science to the point at which it is able to wipe out a whole city by a few explosions of poisonous gas is in a pretty treacherous situation. If the science that it possesses has not helped to found a eutopia, it has at any rate provided the foundations for a kakotopia, or bad place: in short, for a hell. Indeed scientific knowledge has not merely heightened the possibilities of life in the modern world: it has lowered the depths. When science is not touched by a sense of values it works—as it fairly consistently has worked during the past century—towards a complete dehumanization of the social order. The plea that each of the sciences must be permitted to go its own way without control should be immediately rebutted by pointing out that they obviously need a little guidance when their applications in war and industry are so plainly disastrous.

We must be prepared to recognize that "truths" do not stand together on a high and lofty pedestal: some are important and some are trivial, some are innocent and some are dangerous, and while the pursuit of truth is a good in itself—*and complete freedom in that pursuit is a* sine qua non *of a good social life*—certain departments of investigation may need to be offset and corrected by work in other fields. In a modern Western European community, a sociological insight into the causes and conditions of war and peace is a needed corrective to the crudities of applied physical science and without such correction the mere increase of scientific knowledge, of which we boast so vacuously, may be highly inimical to the practice of the good life in the community.

4

If the sciences are to be cultivated anew with respect for a definite hierarchy of human values, it seems to me that the sciences must be focussed again upon particular local communities, and the problems which they offer for solution. Just as geometry in Egypt arose out of the need for annually surveying the boundaries that the Nile wiped out, and as astronomy developed in Chaldea in order to determine the shift of the seasons for the planting of crops, as geology in modern times developed out of the questions that a practical stone mason, like Hugh Miller, found himself confronted with—so may the sciences which are today incomplete and partial develop along the necessary lines by a survey of existing conditions and intellectual resources in a particular community.

On one hand, science must be in contact with the whole idolum of scientific thought—with that vast over-world of scientific effort which is the product of no single place or people or time. On the other hand, it must be related to the definite local community, limited in time and in space, in which its researches and its speculations will be realized and applied. Out of these surveys of existing conditions we should find, I believe, that in social psychology, in anthropology, in economics there are a vast number of facts and relations which remain to be described; and that, similarly, certain departments like craniology and jurisprudence and folklore have been vastly overcultivated in proportion to any genuine importance that their researches may have upon our control over the community's development. Such an investigation would bring out, above all, the weakness of contemporary sociological thought, with its diabetic flatulence of special sociologies, and its lack of any general agreement as to the field which is to be cultivated.

Apart from its great function as a plaything, science is valuable only to the extent that its researches can be brought to bear upon the conditions in a particular community, in a definite region. The difference between science as a plaything and science as an instrument for enabling us to establish more effective relations with other men and with the rest of our environment, is the difference between firing a shot at a target and firing at a buck for provender. The practice one gets in firing at a target is great fun, and incidentally it improves one's marksmanship; such idle sport is per-

[278]

haps one of the stigmata of a civilized community. Nevertheless, unless one's skill can be definitely brought home it remains a personal achievement; and the community as a whole is not a pound of meat the better for it. If science is to play the significant part that Bacon and Andreæ and Plato and the other great humanists desired it to, it must be definitely brought home and realized in our here and now.

The need for this humanization of science has already been perceived in Great Britain. During the last decade a movement has gathered headway in the schools and extended itself to associations outside the schools. The title of this movement is "Regional Survey," and its point of origin is, I believe, the Outlook Tower in Edinburgh which was well described more than two decades ago as the "world's first sociological laboratory."

The aim of the Regional Survey is to take a geographic region and explore it in every aspect. It differs from the social survey with which we are acquainted in America in that it is not chiefly a survey of evils; it is, rather, a survey of the existing conditions in all their aspects; and it emphasizes to a much greater extent than the social survey the natural characteristics of the environment, as they are discovered by the geologist, the zoologist, the ecologist—in addition to the development of natural and human conditions in the historic past, as presented by the anthropologist, the archæologist, and the historian. In short, the regional survey attempts a local synthesis of all the specialist "knowledges."

Such a survey has been conducted in the Southeastern counties of England under the auspices of various local

[279]

scientific societies; and the result of it is a complete description of the community's foundations, its past, its manner of working and living, its institutions, its regional peculiarities, and its utilization of physical, vital, and social resources. Each of the sciences draws upon its general body of knowledge to illuminate the points under observation; and when problems arise which point definitely to the lack of scientific or scholarly data, new trails are opened and new territory defined.

In looking at the community through the Regional Survey, the investigator is dealing with a real thing and not with an arbitrary idolum. In so far as the local community has certain elements in common with similar regions in other countries, or has absorbed elements from other civilizations, these things will be given their full value, instead of being disregarded because they weaken the identity of the local community with that precious myth, the National State. The greater part of the data that is thus brought to light may be plotted on a map, graphically presented in a chart, or photographed. In Saffron Walden, England, there is an admirable little museum devoted to such an exhibition of its region; and in the Outlook Tower, at Edingburgh, there used to be a library and an apparatus of exhibition by which one could begin at the point where one was standing and work outwards, in thought, to embrace the whole wide world. Knowledge that is presented in this fashion is available so that whoever runs may read; it has every feature, therefore, of popular science as it is purveyed in the cheap newspaper and magazine, whilst it remains real science and is not presented as something that verges from a miracle to a superstition.

The knowledge embodied in the Regional Survey has a coherence and pithiness which no isolated study of science can possibly possess. It is presented in such a form that it can be assimilated by every member of the community who has the rudiments of an education, and it thus differs from the isolated discipline which necessarily remains the heritage of the specialist. Above all, this knowledge is not that of "subjects," taken as so many water tight and unrelated compartments: it is a knowledge of a whole region, seen in all its aspects; so that the relations between the work aspect and the soil aspect, between the play aspect and the work aspect, become fairly simple and intelligible. This common tissue of definite, verifiable, localized knowledge is what all our partisan utopias and reconstruction programs have lacked; and lacking it, have been one-sided and ignorant and abstract—devising paper programs for the reconstruction of a paper world.

Regional survey, then, is the bridge by which the specialist whose face is turned towards the library and the laboratory, and the active worker in the field, whose face is turned towards the city and region in which he lives, may come into contact; and out of this contact our plans and our eutopias may be founded on such a permanent foundation of facts as the scientist can build for us, while the sciences themselves will be cultivated with some regard for the human values and standards, as embodied in the needs and the ideals of the local community. This is the first step out of the present impasse: we must return to the real world, and face it, and survey it in its complicated totality. Our castles-in-air must have their foundations in solid ground.

[281]

5

The needed reorientation of science is important; but by itself it is not enough. Knowledge is a tool rather than a motor; and if we know the world without being able to react upon it, we are guilty of that aimless pragmatism which consists of devising all sorts of ingenious machines and being quite incapable of subordinating them to any coherent and attractive pattern.

Now, men are moved by their instinctive impulses and by such emotionally colored pattern-ideas or idola as the dreamer is capable of projecting. When we create these pattern-ideas, we enlarge the environment, so that our behavior is guided by the conditions which we seek to establish and enjoy in an imaginary world. However crude the Marxian analysis of society may have been, it at least had the merit of presenting a great dream—the dream of a titanic struggle between the possessors and the dispossessed in which every worker had a definite part to play. Without these dreams, the advances in social science will be just as disorderly and fusty as the applications of physical science have been in our material affairs, where in the absence of any genuine scale of values, a patent collar button is regarded as equally important as a tungsten filament if the button happens to bring the inventor as great a financial reward.

6

Up to about the middle of the seventeenth century, before modern physical science had rigorously defined its field, the breach between literature and science, which Aristotle had made, was not altogether complete;

[282]

and while the humanist ideal was intact both literature and science were regarded as coeval phases of man's intellectual activity. The two dominating figures of the Renascence, Leonardo da Vinci and Michael Angelo, were artists, technicians, and men of science; and in a comparison between a translation of Michael Angelo's sonnets and a photograph of St. Peter's the sonnets come off rather well.

The great contribution of the Renascence was the ideal of fully energized human beings, able to span life in all its manifestations, as artists, scientists, technicians, philosophers, and what not. This ideal exercised a powerful influence on lesser figures, like the Admirable Crichton and Sir Walter Raleigh, and even down to the time of Descartes it contributed to that exuberance of the intellectual life which was the Renascence at its best. When John Amos Comenius wrote his remarkable little book called The Labyrinth of the World and the Paradise of the Heart in 1623, he combined the outlooks of science and art in a remarkable synthesis; for the first part of this work is a picturesque survey of the actual world as Comenius found it, and the second a picture of the transition to the heavenly world promised in the Christian religion. The idea behind Comenius' Labyrinth was the same that inspired Andreæ; and were it not for the complete otherworldliness of this theological utopia, the Paradise of the Heart, Comenius' discourse would take a high place in the history of utopian thought.

There is no genuine logical basis, as far as I can see, in the dissociation of science and art, of knowing and dreaming, of intellectual activities and emotional activities. The division between the two is simply one of convenience; for both these activities are simply different modes in which human beings create order out of the chaos in which they find themselves. Such is the humanist view. As an instance of this, when the Royal Society was projected in England in the middle of the seventeenth century, Johann Andreæ advised his friend Samuel Hartlib, then in London, not to neglect the humanities while furthering the pursuit of the physical sciences. Unfortunately, the men who gathered together to form the Royal Society were specialists in physical science; and in the lapse of the humanist tradition through the religious acerbities of the time, they had lost some of their desire for a complete life. As a result, the original charter of the society confined its work to the physical sciences.

Insignificant as it now appears in the annals of science, this decision seems to me to mark a definite turning point in human thought. Henceforth the scientist was to be one sort of person and the artist another; henceforth the idolum of science and the idolum of art were not to be cemented together in a single personality; henceforth, in fact, the dehumanization of art and science begins. It is interesting to note that with the divorce of the humanities from science, art and science entered upon separate careers which, for all their diversities, are curiously similar. Both art and science, for example, ceased to be the common property of the community; and each of them split up into a multiplying host of specialisms. In this process, art and science made many notable advances; so that this period is usually spoken of as a period of enlightenment or progress; but the result on the community was what we discovered in our examination of Coketown and the Country House.

7

We must now consider the development of the arts in the modern community. At the height of the Middle Age, as in fifth century Athens, the arts formed together a living unity. A citizen did not go into a concert hall to hear music, to a church to say his prayers, to a theatre to see a play, to a picture gallery to view pictures: it was a mean town, indeed, that could not boast a cathedral and a couple of churches; and in these buildings, drama and music and architecture and painting and sculpture were united for the purpose of ringing changes on the emotional nature of men and converting them to accept the theological vision of otherworldly utopia.

The splitting up of these arts into a number of separate boxes was part of that movement towards individualism and protestantism whose effects most people are familiar with in the field of religion alone. Henceforward, music, drama, painting, and the other arts developed largely in isolation; and each of them was forced to build up a separate world. The greater part of the gains that were made in these worlds was not carried over into the community at large, but remained the possession of the artists themselves or their private patrons and critics in the Country House. With such exceptions as the Italian and Japanese woodcuts of the eighteenth century, and the few survivals of ballad and drama that slipt over from the Middle Age, popular art became another name for all that was coarse and stunted and depressed. The popular architecture

[285]

of the nineteenth century is the sordid little redbrick rabbit hutch: popular religion is embodied in the stunted sheet-iron or brick chapel (as it is called in England) of the Baptists and Methodists: popular music is the latest barrel organ lilt: popular painting is the calendar lithograph: and popular literature is the dime novel.

The divorce of the art of the cultivated classes from that of the whole community tended to deprive it of any other standards than the artist himself was content to erect. Here again the comparison with science is curiously pertinent. The world of art is in a sense a separate world, and it can be cultivated for a time without reference to the desires and emotions of the community out of which it has sprung. But the motto "Art for art's sake" turns out in practice to be something quite different—namely, art for the artist's sake; and art which is produced in this manner, without any external standard of performance, is frequently just an instrument for overcoming a neurosis or enabling the artist to restore his personal equilibrium. Divorced from his community, the artist was driven back upon himself: instead of seeking to create a beauty which all men might share, he devoted himself to projecting a poignant angle of his personal vision—an angle which I shall call the picturesque. The cause of this divorce I have already pointed out in the chapter on the Country House; it is with the effects of this divorce, for which the artist was not greatly to blame, that we are here concerned.

This conflict between "beauty" and the "picturesque" is perhaps common to all the arts, and with sufficient factual detail I might be able to trace its effects on literature and music. For the sake of clearness and simplicity I shall confine myself to painting and sculpture, with the proviso that our conclusions will apply, by and large, to the whole field.

Let me emphasize, before going any further, that I am using the terms "beauty" and the "picturesque" in quite different senses from the vague ones that are usually attached to them; and that I use them without any preliminary judgment as to their place and value in the good life. The picturesque, in the quite arbitrary sense in which the word is used here, is an abstract quality of vision, sound, or meaning which creates what we might call pure esthetic experience. In painting, the picturesque probably arose with the discovery, on the part of the leisured classes in the Country House, that it was possible to achieve rapture, a sort of esthetic trance, a complete state of beatitude, by the more or less prolonged contemplation of a pictorial subject. Up to the time of this discovery, painting was simply a branch of interior decoration; the great paintings of the Christian World served, for the public, as illustrations to that outline of history which mediæval theology provided: they had a habitat, a social destination.

With the splitting off of the picturesque from the main body of ecclesiastical art, painting came into its own as an end in itself, apart from any place that it might have in the scheme of the community's affairs. The symptom of this change is the rise of landscape painting: in the search for pure esthetic experience the painter began to look for themes which were divorced from any human interest but that of pure contemplation. During the last century this split between painting as a form of social art and painting as a means of achieving contemplative ecstasy has become deeper: even those academic painters who followed the methods of the older artists no longer have the same field to work in, whilst the revolutionist—the impressionists of one period, the cubists of another, and the post-impressionists or expressionists of a third—are forced by the general irrelevance of art in Coketown to produce work which only the more or less initiate will appreciate.

Now, I would not for worlds underrate the gains which have been achieved by the divorce of art from the whole life of the community. In their isolation from the social group that produced them the modern artists have been able to pursue their solitary way to limits which the common man is probably incapable of reaching: they have widened the field of esthetic delight and have introduced new values into the world of painting, values which will remain even though the disease which created them disappears, just as one can salvage a pearl from an oyster whose sickness is healed. The view from the mountain top is none the worse because many people are afflicted with dizziness and nausea before they have reached the summit; and, like the pursuit of truth, the pursuit of esthetic values is a good in itself apart from any values which may be realized in the community. On these terms, Cézanne and Van Gogh and Ryder, to mention a few of the dead, will hold their own, and keep the boundaries of art from ever shrinking again, I trust, to its academic limits.

Nevertheless, the effects of focussing on the pictur-

esque can no more be overlooked in art than the danger
of specialization in science. It is almost a banality
to point out how, historically, as the picturesque developed in art, beauty has tended to disappear from life.
Whilst the cultivated few have become gloriously alive
to more exquisite sensations than their ancestors had
probably ever experienced, the "mutilated many" have
been forced to live in great cities and in abject country
towns of a blackness and ugliness such as the world,
if we are to judge by the records that exist, has never
seen before. In other words, we have become more sensitive to experiences—to the contents of our inner worlds
—only to become more callous to things, to the brash
surfaces of the world without. In our preoccupation
with the inner worlds we have to a large extent lost
our hold upon beauty, which, in the limiting sense in
which the word is used here, is the quality by which
anything, from a torso to a building, shows its adaptation to an end and its sensitiveness to esthetic values—
values which are abstracted and intensified in the pure
picturesque—that are involved in such an adaptation.
In this sense, the beautiful, as Emerson said, rests on
the foundations of the necessary: it is the outward
token of an inward grace; its appearance is the mani-
festation of a humanized life; and its existence and
development constitute, in fact, a sort of index to
community's vitality.

The divorce of the artist from the community, and
the turning away of his energies from beauty, in which
the picturesque might be fulfilled, to the picturesque
itself, separate from any practical needs, has scarcely
been compensated by the advances that have been made
in the separate world of art. The result has been that

[289]

work which should have been done by artists of great capacity has been done by people of minor or degraded ability. Anonymous jerrybuilders have erected the greater number of our houses, absurd engineers have laid out our towns with no thought for anything but sewers and paving contracts; rapacious and illiterate men who have achieved success in business discourse to the multitude on what constitutes the good life—and so on. There is really no end to the number of things which we do badly in the modern community, for want of the artist to do them at all.

This generalization applies to the whole range of the arts. The greater part of the creative dreaming and planning which constitutes literature and art has had very little bearing upon the community in which we live, and has done little to equip us with patterns, with images and ideals, by means of which we might react creatively upon our environment. Yet it should be obvious that if the inspiration for the good life is to come from anywhere, it must come from no other people than the great artists. An intense social life, as Gabriel Tarde pointed out in his fine utopian fantasy, Underground Man, has "for its indispensable condition the esthetic life and the universal propagation of the religion of truth and beauty." The common man, when he is in love, has a little glimpse of the way in which the drudgery of the daily world may be transmuted through emotional stimulus; it is the business of the artist to make the transmutation permanent, for the only difference between the artist and the common man is that the artist is, so to say, in love all the while. It is out of the vivid patterns of the artist's ecstasy that he draws men together and gives them the vision to

[290]

shape their lives and the destiny of their community anew.

8

No matter how the modern artist may use or fritter away his abilities, it is plain that he has an enormous reservoir of power at his disposal. What, for instance, has made America so wholly devoted to the conquest of material things? Why are we so given over to collecting those vast miscellanies of goods which are temptingly displayed in the advertising sections of our illustrated weeklies and monthly magazines? The necessity for ameliorating the hard, crude life of the pioneer has indeed been an important influence; but the traditions of this life in turn produced all the minor "artists" or "artlings" who write and draw for the popular papers, who create the plots of plays and motion picture scenarios; and since most of these poor wretches have never been educated in the humanist sense to any degree—since they know no other environment than New York or Los Angeles or Gopher Prairie, since they are acquainted with the achievements of no other age than their own, they have devoted themselves wholeheartedly to idealizing a great many of the things that are crude or ugly or stupid in their beloved community. So the idola of business have been perpetuated by "artlings" who themselves know only the standards of the business man.

Because of the limited horizons of the American artist, therefore, the rising generation aspires after the things that Messrs. Jack London, Rupert Hughes, Scott Fitzgerald, and heaven knows who else have thought good and fine; the younger generation talks

like the heroes and heroines of a melodrama by Mr.
Samuel Shipman, when they do not attain the higher
level of comic cuts; the younger generation thrills to
the type of beauty which Mr. Penryhn Stanlaws sets before its gaze. The notion that the common man de-
spises art is absurd. The common man worships art
and lives by it; and when good art is not available he
takes the second best or the tenth best or the hundredth
best. The success of Mr. Eugene O'Neil, one of the few
playwrights of any girth who has contributed to the
American stage, proves that the only way that people
can be kept away from good art is by not providing it.
The younger generation might just as well have had
its idea-patterns shaped by Sophocles, Praxiteles, and
Plato, if our genuine artists were not so aloof to their
responsibilities, and if they were intellectually mature
enough to accept the full burden of their vocation. It
is a sign of a terrific neurosis—and no mark at all of
esthetic aptitude—that our genuine art is so completely disoriented and so thoroughly out of touch with
the community. We must turn to a man of such
uneven parts as Mr. Nicholas Vachel Lindsay before
we have anything like a recognition of the classic rôle
of the artist.

Art for the artist's sake is largely a symptom of that
neurotic individualism which drives the artist out of a
public world which baffles him into a private world
where he may reign in solitude as an unruly demiurge.
Art for the public's sake, on the other hand, substitutes the vices of the extrovert for the vices of the
introvert. When I say that art must have some vital
contact with the community I do not mean, let me
emphasize, that the artist must cater to public whim

[292]

or demand. Art in its social setting is neither a personal cathartic for the artist, nor a salve to quiet the
itching vanity of the community: it is essentially a
means by which people who have had a strange diversity of experiences have their activities emotionally
canalized into patterns and molds which they are able
to share pretty completely with each other. Pure
art is inevitably propaganda. I mean by this that it
is meant to be propagated, and that in so far as it
fails to impregnate the community in which it exists
with its ideas and images, in so far as the community
is not changed for better or worse by its existence, its
claims are spurious. Propagandist art, on the other
hand, is inevitably impure since instead of bringing
people together on a common emotional plane, as men,
it tends to accentuate their differences, and to void
emotions which are proper to art into a realm where
the emotions of the missionary's tent or the soap-
boxer's platform hold exclusive sway. It is just because the "artist" in America has been impure in
motive—a propagandist for Pollyanna in the face of
Euripides, a propagandist for "just folks" in the face
of Swift, a propagandist for niceness in the face of
Rabelais—that he has failed miserably as an artist,
and has left our communities to stew so completely in
their own savorless juice.

9

For examples of what the artist might be, and what
his proper relation to the community might be when
he was mature enough to recognize it and discipline
himself to it, let us look at Mr. William Butler Yeats
or A.E. There are doubtless a good many other exam-

ples that might be offered in Europe; but these are
particularly good; for the reason that with A.E. one
can see in his The National Being how the conceptions
of art enter into the tissues of all his plans for renovating life in the Irish Countryside. In the work of these
artists and their fellows we have a clue to one of the
most promising attempts to establish a concrete eutopia
which shall rise out of the real facts of the everyday
environment and, at the same time, turn upon them
and mold them creatively a little nearer the heart's
desire.

In the account of Four Years which Mr. Yeats
published in The Dial he explains his attitude towards
the literature and social life of Ireland; and I recom-
mend that account to all the forlorn revolutionaries
and reformers who wonder why the dry bones of their
doctrines remain dry bones, instead of knitting themselves together and becoming alive. This passage in
particular, defines the relation of the artist both to
the tradition of his art and to the community in which
he must find a root:

"The Huxley, Tyndall, Carolus Duran, Bastien-
Lepage coven, asserted that an artist or a poet must
paint or write in the style of his own day, and this with
the Fairy Queen and the Lyrical Ballads and Blake's
early poems in its ears, and plain to the eyes, in book
and gallery, those great masterpieces of later Egypt,
founded upon that work of the ancient kingdom already
further in time from Later Egypt than Later Egypt is
from us." He dismisses this claim with the just assertion that the artist is free to choose any style that suits
his mood and subject; for in the world of art time and
space are irrelevant; and he goes on to say, "We had in

Ireland imaginative stories, which the uneducated classes knew and even sang, and might we not make those stories current among the educated classes, rediscovering, for the work's sake, what I have called 'the applied arts of literature,' the association of literature, that is, with music, speech, and dance; and at last, it might be, so deepen the political passion of the nation that all, artist and poet, craftsman and day laborer, would accept a common design. Perhaps even these images, once created and associated with river and mountain, might move of themselves and with some powerful, even turbulent life, like those painted horses that trample the rice-fields of Japan."

By citing Mr. Yeats' conceptions I do not mean to limit the artist to a single function—that of patterning the good life. It is quite plain that pure esthetic experience is a good in itself; and when the artist has rendered this experience in a picture, a poem, a novel, a philosophy, he has performed a unique and indispensable piece of work. Could italics keep this passage from being ignored I should employ them.

What I have called the picturesque is in reality just as self-sustaining and delightful as the radiant good health which Sir Thomas More rated so highly in his Utopia. If the community went to the dogs, it would still be exuberantly self-sustaining, whilst anyone had the time or the capacity to enjoy it. What I protest against is the way in which the field of the genuine artist, during these last three hundred years, has been whittled away, so that it has become more and more a mark of the artist to concern himself solely with the narrow province of pure esthetic experience, and to protest his complete aloofness from anything that lies

[295]

outside this realm. Such an attitude would have struck Euripides or Milton or Goethe or Wagner as undignified and stupid, I am sure, because art is as large as life, and it does not gain in vigor or intensity by reducing its scope to that of the puppet stage. The point is that there is an artistic function to be performed in the community, for the community, as well as in the world of art, for those who are lifted up to art.

"Nations, races, and individual men," as Mr. Yeats says again, "are unified by an image, or a bundle of related images, symbolical and provocative of the state of mind that is, of all states of mind not impossible, the most difficult to that man, race, or nation; because only the greatest obstacle that can be contemplated without despair rouses the will to full intensity."

Whether these images shall be provided by patrioteers, hack editors, politicians, advertising men and commercialized "artists" or whether they shall be created by genuine playwrights and poets and philosophers is an important question. The function of creating these images is an artistic one, and the artist who evades his responsibility is making life for himself and his kind more difficult, since in the long run a community whose sacred literature is written by Colonel Diver and Scadder and Jefferson Brick—the great heroes of Civilization as the star of empire westward makes its way—will make even the most solitary cultivation of the arts a thorny and difficult task.

In the good life, the purely esthetic element has a prominent place; but unless the artist is capable of moving men to the good life, the esthetic element is bound to be driven farther and farther away from the common realities, until the world of the artist will

[296]

scarcely be distinguishable from the phantasia of dementia præcox. Already, the symptoms of this corrosive **futility** have appeared in literature and painting in Western Europe and America; and such light as comes forth from this art is but the phosphorescence of decay. If the arts are not to disintegrate utterly, must they not focus more and more upon eutopia?

10

It comes to this then: our plans for a new social order have been as dull as mud because, in the first place, they have been abstract and cockney, and have not taken into account the immense diversity and complexity of man's environment; and in the second place, they have not created any vivid patterns that would move men to great things. They have not been "informed by science and ennobled by the arts."

Through the paralysis of the arts and sciences our contemporary programs for revolution and reform have done very little to lift our heads over the disorderly and bedraggled environments in which we conduct our daily business. This failure to create a common pattern for the good life in each region has made such excellent efforts as the garden city movement seem weak and ineffectual when we place them alongside the towns that mediæval civilization, which had such a common pattern, created. Without the common background of eutopian idola, all our efforts at rehabilitation—the new architecture, the garden city movement, the electrification of industry, the organization of great industrial guilds such as the Building Trades have achieved in England and the garment workers seem on the point of effecting

in America—without these common idola, I say, all
our practical efforts are spotty and inconsecutive and
incomplete. It was not, let us remember, by any legislative device that the cities of the industrial age were
monotonously patterned in the image of Coketown. It
was rather because everyone within these horrid centers accepted the same values and pursued the same
ends—as they were projected by economists like
Ricardo, industrialists like Stephenson, and lyric poets
like Samuel Smiles—that the plans of the jerrybuilder
and the engineer expressed to perfection the brutality
and social disharmony of the community. The same
process that gave us Coketown can, when our world of
ideas is transformed, give us something better than
Coketown.

The chief use of the classic utopias that we have
surveyed is to suggest that the same methods which
are used by the utopian thinkers to project an ideal
community on paper may be employed, in a practical
way, to develop a better community on earth. The
weakness of the utopian thinkers consisted in the assumption that the dreams and projects of any single
man might be realized in society at large. From the
bitter frustration of Fourier, Cabet, Hertzka, and even
John Ruskin those who are in search of the beloved
community may well take a warning. Where the critics
of the utopian method were, I believe, wrong was in holding that the business of projecting prouder worlds
was a futile and footling pastime. These anti-utopian
critics overlooked the fact that one of the main factors
that condition any future are the attitudes and beliefs
which people have in relation to that future—that, as
Mr. John Dewey would say, in any judgment of prac-

tise one's belief in a hypothesis is one of the things that affect its realization.

When we have projected the pattern of an ideal community and tend to warp our conduct in conformity with that pattern, we overcome the momentum of actual institutions. In feeling free to project new patterns, in holding that human beings can will a change in their institutions and habits of life, the utopians were, I believe, on solid ground; and the utopian philosophies were a great improvement over the more nebulous religious and ethical systems of the past in that they saw the necessity for giving their ideals form and life. In fact, it has been in the pictures of ideal commonwealths such as Plato's that the "ideal" and the "actual" have met.

It is true that the pure utopians have overlooked the fact that every institution has a momentum of its own: its speed may be quickened or reduced, it may be switched on another track, as the Roman Church during the Reformation was switched from the main line of civilization to a subsidiary route; and at times, in the catastrophe of war or revolution, an institution may jump the track altogether and be wrecked. The critical problem for the eutopian, the problem of the transition from one set of institutions to another, from one way of life to another, was overlooked. Plato's Republic, for example, was a fairly attractive place; but one wonders in what Greek city in the Fourth Century B.C. the transition could have taken place. A transition implies not merely a goal but a starting point: if we are to move the world, as Archimedes threatened to with his lever, we must have some ground to stand on. It is only by paying attention to the nitations of each region, and by allowing for the riving force of history, that we can make the earth come to terms with man's idola. This is perhaps the most difficult lesson that the eutopian must learn.

11

What, then, is the first step out of the present disorder? The first step, it seems to me, is to ignore all the fake utopias and social myths that have proved either so sterile or so disastrous during the last few centuries. There is perhaps no logical reason why the myth of the national state should not be preserved; but it is a myth which has done very little, on the whole, to promote the good life, and has on the contrary done a great deal to make the good life impossible; and to continue to cling to it in the face of perpetual wars, pestilences, and spiritual devastations is the sort of fanaticism which will probably seem as blind and cruel to future generations as persecutions for Christian heresy do to the present one. On the same grounds, there are a number of other social myths, like the proletarian myth, which run so badly against the grain of reality that they cannot be preserved without ignoring a great many values which are essential to a humane existence; and on pragmatic grounds it would be fine and beneficial to drop them quickly into limbo. There is no reason to think that there will be a quick conversion from these myths: the holocaust of war has only intensified the myth of the National State; and our experience with religious myths suggests on the contrary that the forms at any rate will be preserved long after the last shred of reality has disappeared. But the sooner those who are capable of intellectual criti-

[300]

cism abandon these particular myths, the sooner will these idola fall into the state which has been happily described as "innocuous desuetude."

If our knowledge of human behavior counts for anything, however, we cannot put aside old myths without creating new ones. The eighteenth century agnostics very wisely realized that if they wished to maintain the values which had been created by Deism, they could not abandon God without inventing him all over again. In turning away from obsolete and disastrous social myths I do not suggest that we give up the habit of making myths; for that habit, for good or bad, seems to be ingrained in the human psyche. The nearest we can get to rationality is not to efface our myths but to attempt to infuse them with right reason, and to alter them or exchange them for other myths when they appear to work badly.

Here is where we reap the full benefit of the great utopian tradition. In turning away from the social myths that hamper us, we do not jump blindly into a blankness: we rather ally ourselves with a different order of social myth which has always been vivified and enriched by the arts and sciences.

The idolum of eutopia which we may seek to project in this or that region is not a *carte blanche* which any one may fill in at his will and caprice; certain lines have already been fixed; certain spaces have already been filled. There is a consensus among all utopian writers, to begin with, that the land and natural resources belong undividedly to the community; and even when it is worked by separate people or associations, as in Utopia and Freeland the increment of the land—the economic rent—belongs to the community as a whole.

[301]

There is also a pretty common notion among the utopians that, as land is a common possession, so is work
a common function; and no one is let off from some
sort of labor of body or mind because of any inherited
privileges or dignities that he can point to.   Finally,
there is the almost equally common notion, among the
utopians, that the perpetuation of the species leaves
plenty of room for improvement, and that, as far as
human knowledge and foresight are worth anything, it
should be applied to propagation; so that the most reck-
less and ill-bred shall not burden the community with
the support of their offspring while those of finer
capacity are neglected or overwhelmed in numbers.

Besides these general conditions for the good life
which the utopians unite to emphasize, there are certain
other points in the utopian tradition of which one
writer or another has given the classic statement.

With Plato we see the enormous importance of birth
and education; we recognize the part good breeding,
in every sense of the word, must play in the good community.   Sir Thomas More makes us aware of the fact
that a community becomes a community to the extent
that it has shared possessions, and he suggests that the
local group might develop such a common life as the
old colleges of Oxford have enjoyed.   When we turn to
Christianopolis, we are reminded that the daily life and
work of the community must be infused with the spirit
of science, and that an acute practical intelligence such
as we find today among the engineers need not be
divorced from the practice of the humanities.   Even the
nineteenth century utopias have a contribution to make.
They remind us by their overemphasis that all the proud
and mighty idealisms in the world are so many shadows

unless they are supported by the whole economic fabric
—so that "eutopia" is not merely a matter of spiritual
conversion, as the ancient religions taught, but of economic and geotechnic reconstruction. Finally, from
James Buckingham and Ebenezer Howard we can learn
the importance of converting the idolum of eutopia into
plans and layouts and detailed projections, such as a
townplanner might utilize; and we may suspect that a
eutopia which cannot be converted into such specific
plans will continue, as the saying is, to remain up in
the air.

Taken together, there is a powerful impulse towards
creating a good environment for the good life in the
classic utopias we have examined: from one or another
utopia we may draw elements which will enrich every
part of the community's life. By following the utopian
tradition we shall not merely escape from the fake
utopias that have dominated us: we shall return to
reality. More than that, we shall return upon reality
and perhaps—who can tell?—we shall re-create it!

12

In discussing the foundations of Eutopia I am conscious of a certain abstractness in my method of argument; conscious that I have not been a good utopian
in dealing with these proud idola that we may project
in every region. Let us come down to earth now and
realize what all this amounts to when we turn away
from the library and mingle again on the highways that
lead past our door.

First of all, I conceive that we shall not attempt to
envisage a single utopia for a single unit called humanity; that is the sort of thin and tepid abstraction

[303]

which the discipline of the Regional Survey will tend to kill off even in people who are now inured by education to dealing only in verbal things. All the human beings on the planet are a unity only for the sake of talking about them; and as far as that goes, there is very little profitable conversation that can apply to a Greenlander, a Parisian, and a Chinaman, except the mere observation that they are all on the same little boat of a planet and would probably be much happier if they minded their own business and were not too insistent about inflicting their institutions and their idola upon their neighbors.

We shall have to dismiss, as equally futile, the notion of a single stratification of mankind, such as the working class, serving as the foundation for our Eutopia: the notion that the working class consists simply of urban workers is a cockney imbecility, and as soon as one rectifies it and includes the agricultural population, we have "humanity" pretty much all over again. Finally, if we are to give eutopia a local habitation it will not be founded upon the National State, for the National State is a myth which sane people will no more sacrifice their lives to than they would hand their children into the furnace of some tribal Moloch; and a good idolum cannot be founded on the basis of a bad one.

As far as extent or character of territory goes, we will remember that the planet is not as smooth as a billiard ball, and that the limits of any genuine community rest within fairly ascertainable geographic regions in which a certain complex of soil, climate, industry, institutional life and historic heritage has prevailed. We shall not attempt to legislate for all these communities at one stroke; for we shall respect William Blake's dictum that one law for the lion and the ox is tyranny. There are some 15,000,000 local communities in the world, the Postal Directory tells us; and our eutopia will necessarily take root in one of these real communities, and include within its co-operations as many other communities, as have similar interests and identities. It may be that our eutopia will embrace a population as great as that in the Metropolis of London or New York; but it is needless to say that the land which lies beyond the limits of the metropolis will no longer be regarded as a sort of subterranean factory for the production of agricultural goods. In sum, as Patrick Geddes has finely said, in the Kingdom of Eutopia—the world Eutopia—there will be many mansions.

The inhabitants of our eutopias will have a familiarity with their local environment and its resources, and a sense of historic continuity, which those who dwell within the paper world of Megalopolis and who touch their environment mainly through the newspaper and the printed book, have completely lost. The people of Newcastle will no longer go to London for coals, as the people in the provinces have in a sense been doing this last century and more: there will be a more direct utilization of local resources than would have seemed profitable or seemly to the metropolitan world which now has command of the market. In these varied eutopias, it is safe to say, there will be a new realization of the fact that a cultivated life is essentially a settled life: their citizens will have discovered that the great privilege of travelling from Brooklyn to Bermondsey, and from Bermondsey to Bombay is scarcely worth the trouble when the institutions of Brooklyn, Bermondsey, and Bombay, and every other purely industrial center, are identical—sanitary drinking devices and canned goods and moving pictures being the same wherever mechanical duplication of goods for a world market has taken the place of direct adaptation to local needs.

It should not surprise us therefore if the foundations of eutopia were established in ruined countries; that is, in countries where metropolitan civilization has collapsed and where all its paper prestige is no longer accepted at its paper value. There was the beginning of a genuine eutopian movement in Denmark after the war with Germany in the 'sixties: under the leadership of Bishop Gruntwig came a revival of folk traditions in literature and a renascence of education which has renewed the life of the Danish countryside and made an intelligent farmer and an educated man out of the boor. It would not be altogether without precedent if such a eutopian renascence took place in Germany, in Austria, in Russia; and perhaps on another scale in India and China and Palestine; for all these regions are now face to face with realities which the "prosperous" paperism of our metropolitan civilization has largely neglected.

If the inhabitants of our Eutopias will conduct their daily affairs in a possibly more limited environment than that of the great metropolitan centers, their mental environment will not be localized or nationalized. For the first time perhaps in the history of the planet our advance in science and invention has made it possible for every age and every community to contribute to the spiritual heritage of the local group; and the citizen

[306]

of eutopia will not stultify himself by being, let us say, a hundred per cent Frenchman when Greece, China, England, Scandinavia and Russia can give sustenance to his spiritual life. Our eutopians will necessarily draw from this wider environment whatever can be assimilated by the local community; and they will thus add any elements that may be lacking in the natural situation.

The chief business of eutopians was summed up by Voltaire in the final injunction of Candide: Let us cultivate our garden. The aim of the real eutopian is the culture of his environment, most distinctly not the culture, and above all not the exploitation, of some other person's environment. Hence the size of our Eutopia may be big or little; it may begin in a single village; it may embrace a whole region. A little leaven will leaven the whole loaf; and if a genuine pattern for the eutopian life plants itself in any particular locality it may ramify over a whole continent as easily as Coketown duplicated itself throughout the Western World. The notion that no effective change can be brought about in society until millions of people have deliberated upon it and willed it is one of the rationalizations which are dear to the lazy and the ineffectual. Since the first step towards eutopia is the reconstruction of our idola, the foundations for eutopia can be laid, wherever we are, without further ado.

Our most important task at the present moment is to build castles in the air. We need not fear, as Thoreau reminds us, that the work will be lost. If our eutopias spring out of the realities of our environment, it will be easy enough to place foundations under them. Without a common design, without a grand design, all

[307]

our little bricks of reconstruction might just as well remain in the brickyard; for a disharmony between men's minds betokens, in the end, the speedy dilapidation of whatever they may build. Our final word is a counsel of perfection. When that which is perfect has come, that which is imperfect will pass away. ✓

BIBLIOGRAPHY

For the benefit of the reader who wishes to travel further along the trails opened up in this survey of utopias, I am giving a list of the principal books on the subject. This list includes all the important utopias that are accessible in English, as well as a few that are not; but it is not exhaustive, for the region of Utopia has its swamps and arid places as well as its fertile and cultivated land; and no one but a scholarly explorer need attempt to enter the more forbidding parts of the country.

Needless to say, in dealing with our historic utopias I had a rough criterion of selection. I set out to treat such plans for the improvement of the human community as had been embodied in complete pictures of an ideal commonwealth: this excluded important essays in politics like Hobbes' Leviathan and Harrington's Oceana; and it ruled out any treatment of abstract idealisms which, however important, did not exemplify the essential utopian method. Next, I resolved to deal at length only with those utopias which have exercised some influence on thought and life, particularly in the Western European world. Third, I sought to emphasize what was common in the methods and ends of the classic utopias; making plain their relations within the world of utopias and their relevance in the present day, rather than attempting to show in any detail the social milieu in which each utopian wrote. In dealing with the nineteenth century my criterion became a little shaky; and I frankly chose the nineteenth century utopias on the basis of their association with temporal movements like state socialism, the single tax, and syndicalism, rather

[309]

than because of their conformity to standards which served to weed out irrelevant utopias in the earlier centuries. In devoting a little space to Fourier and Spence and giving short shrift to Owen I have tried to restore these interesting and significant figures to the place that they deserve. There will doubtless be disagreements over my selections and the amount of space I have allotted to various writers; but at least, where there has been madness there has also been method.

Certain parts of the argument are not covered by this list of utopias. The best introductions to utopian literature in general are in German; see R. Blueher's excellent pamphlet on Moderne Utopien; Ein Beitrag zur Geschichte des Sozialismus, Bonn: 1920. While Mr. Van Wyck Brooks put me independently on the trail of Rabelais' Abbey of Theleme I must acknowledge, with as much grace as possible, that Herr Blueher anticipated me in grasping this clue to Renascence culture; and if any credit is due, he deserves it. The most exhaustive catalogue of pre-nineteenth century utopias is contained in Kautsky's Vorläufer des Modernen Sozialismus. Max Beer's History of British Socialism has an excellent discussion of the relation of the utopians to socialism. See also Moritz Kaufmann's Utopias; or Schemes of Social Improvement, from Sir Thomas More to Karl Marx, London: 1879. In the excellent History of Utopian Thought, by Dr. J. O. Hertzler (Macmillan: 1923), the phantasists are sympathetically treated.

The chapter on the Country House might well be prefaced by Mr. Thorstein Veblen's Theory of the Leisure Class, a satire which seems to me unique in scholarship and originality. The importance of our social myths and our collective representations has been noted by a whole school of French sociologists who follow Émile Durkheim; and the dynamic force of ideas has been treated by Alfred Fouillée. On both these topics there is a whole literature;

and it would give a sense of false simplicity to single out any particular essay. There is a fairly popular discussion of the place of myths and ideals in the George Sorel's Reflexions on Violence, and Benjamin Kidd's Science of Power (especially Chapter V.).

As a loose illustration of the general method and outlook embodied in this book I refer to the Making of the Future Series, edited by Messrs. Patrick Geddes and Victor Branford and published by Williams & Norgate, London. There is an able exposition of the regionalist movement and of the fundamental realities upon which this movement is based in two books published in that series; namely, Professor Fleure's Human Geography in Western Europe and C. B. Fawcett's The Provinces of England. Two works by the editors, The Coming Polity and Our Social Inheritance are likewise suggestive. Professor Geddes is the outstanding exponent of the Eutopian method both in thought and in practical activity; and the reader should consult his City Development (1904) and his Town-Planning towards City Development: a Report to the Durbar of Indore, 2 vols. Indore, 1918. Both of these books are mines from which all sorts of precious thoughts can be quarried. Remaindered copies of the first can be obtained from John Grant, Bookseller, Edinburgh; while the second is sold by Botsford, High Holborn, London. Professor Geddes' work exemplifies concretely a good part of what I have sought to explain and define in not altogether adequate prose.

UTOPIAS

Plato (427 B. C.-347 B. C.). The Republic. Translated with notes and essays by Benjamin Jowett. Oxford: 1894. See also Plato's Critias and Statesman in the same edition. The Laws, which is a more detailed attempt to work out the details of a good polity, is so lacking in Plato's original inspiration that, but for Aristotle's allusion to it, one would promptly take it for the work of another hand.

More, Sir Thomas (1478-1535). Utopia. Published originally in Latin in 1516. There are numerous modern editions. See Ideal Commonwealths, edited by Henry Morley.

Andreæ, Johann Valentin (1586-1654). Christianopolis. Published in 1619 and translated in 1916 by Felix Emil Held under the title of Christianopolis: An Ideal State of the 17th Century. Oxford University Press. Mr. Held's introduction contains an account of Andreæ's life.

Bacon, Francis (1561-1626). The New Atlantis. Published in 1627. Bacon contemplated writing a second part which would deal with the laws of his ideal commonwealth. See Ideal Commonwealths.

Campanella, Tomasso (1568-1639). The City of the Sun. Published in 1637 as Civitas Solis Poetica: Idea Reipublicæ Philosophiæ. See Ideal Commonwealths.

[312]

ALLAIS, DENIS VAIRASSE D' (—). L'Histoire des Sevaram-
bes. Written in 1672 and translated into English as
The History of the Sevarites, written by one Captain
Siden, London: 1675. In Kautsky's Vorläufer des
Modernen Sozialismus this utopia is given high praise
and is ranked as the French parallel of More's Utopia;
but I feel that this is a sad error in judgment which
perhaps arose out of the bare fact that the first law of
the great dictator Sevarias was to put all private property in the hands of the state, to be disposed of absolutely by its authority, and to do away with distinctions
of rank and hereditary dignity. There is little that is
fresh or imaginative in Vairasse's treatment, however,
and there is nothing like More's detailed effort to
guard against usurpation of power by the ruling
classes. As simple fiction, the History of the Sevarites
is, however, readable. See also L'Histoire des Gal-
ligènes, by Tiphaigne de la Roche; likewise the excellent satire, Giphantia. The description of Salen-
tum, under Mentor, in Fénélon's Telemachus should
not be neglected. The Abbé Morelly's Basiliade is
little more than a definition of his Code de la Nature.

MERCIER, LOUIS SEBASTIEN (1740-1814). Memoirs of the
Year 2500. Published in French in 1772 and translated into English, Liverpool: 1802.

SPENCE, THOMAS (1750-1814). Description of Spensonia.
Constitution of Spensonia. London: 1795. Privately
printed at the Courier Press; Leamington Spa: 1917.

FOURIER, CHARLES FRANÇOIS MARIE (1772-1837). Traité
de l'Association domestique agricole. 2 vols. 1822.
Le Nouveau Monde Industriel. 2 vols. 1829. See
also Albert Brisbane in his General Introduction to
the Social Sciences (Fourier's "Social Destinies"),
and Selections from the Works of Fourier, translated

by Julia Franklin, with an introduction by Charles Gide, London: 1901.

CABET, ÉTIENNE (1788-1856). Voyage en Icarie. Published in 1845 and numerous editions followed during the next five years; see that of the Bureau du Populaie, Paris: 1848.

BUCKINGHAM, JAMES SILK (1786-1855). National Evils and Practical Remedies, with a plan for a model town. London: 1848.

BULWER-LYTTON, E. (1803-1873). The Coming Race; or the New Utopia. London: 185—. A fantastic romance about a people who live underground, possess detachable wings, and command a potency known as "vril." It is perhaps not altogether without significance that this new hierarchy of industrial angels was conceived by Lytton in the same decade that saw the building of the Crystal Palace.

PEMBERTON, ROBERT (—). The Happy Colony. London: 1854. This is an appeal to the working class, somewhat similar in temper and method to Buckingham's appeal to the middle class. Pemberton had an individual system of psychology which he desired to apply in education. This utopia has now only a limited historical significance.

BELLAMY, EDWARD (1850-1898). Looking Backward; Boston: 1888. Equality; Boston: 1897.

HERTZKA, THEODOR (1845-?). Freeland: A Social Anticipation. First edition published in German, 1889; English translation published by the British Freeland Association in 1891. A Visit to Freeland, or the New Paradise Regained. Translation published by the above Association, London: 1894. The first work lays the foundations for the utopia; the second is the ideal commonwealth in action.

MORRIS, WILLIAM (1834-1896). News from Nowhere. London: 1890. There have been numerous editions.

HOWARD, EBENEZER (1850-?). Garden Cities of Tomorrow. London: 1902. First published as Tomorrow in 1898. Unique among utopian books in that its eutopia has been partly realized. See numerous descriptions of Letchworth, the first Garden City.

HUDSON, W. H. (—). A Crystal Age. London: 1906.

THIRION, EMILE (1825-?). Neustria: Utopie Individualiste. Paris: 1901. This is one of the rare, deliberately individualistic utopias, founded on work, liberty, and property. It assumes that a colony of Girondists were able to establish themselves in South America.

HERZL, THEODOR (1860–1904). Altneuland. Leipzig: 1903.

TARDE, GABRIEL (1843-1904). Underground Man. London: 1905. A deft and well-conceived fantasy, full of excellent criticism. Towards the past it is a utopia of reconstruction, towards the future—but herein lies much of its charm!—it is one of escape.

WELLS, H. G. (1866-?). A Modern Utopia. New York: 1905.

CRAM, RALPH ADAMS (1863-?). Walled Towns. Boston: 1919. Dr. Cram does not classify this work as a utopia; but the honest critic cannot help giving it that label. Dr. Cram sees no basis for eutopia without the system of values and the sanctions perpetuated by the Christian Church; since this leaves the greater part of humanity in Darkness, I cannot agree with him. Dr. Cram, however, is a fine scholar and a stimulating critic; and if one could only grant his assumptions his conclusions would be magnificent.

MORLEY, HENRY. Ideal Commonwealths; Plutarch's Lycurgus, More's Utopia, Bacon's New Atlantis, Campanella's City of the Sun, and a Fragment of Hall's Mundus Alter et Idem, with an introduction by Henry Morley. London: G. Routledge, 1886.